ProActive Selling

Control the Process—
Win the Sale

William "Skip" Miller

AMACOM
American Management Association
New York • Atlanta • Brussels • Buenos Aires • Chicago • London • Mexico City
San Francisco •Shanghai • Tokyo • Toronto • Washington, D. C.

To all who have tried and tried, and finally succeeded. You have taken a risk, faced
fear in the eye, and then wondered why you had that fear, and what took you so long.

To all who have not yet tried. You will face that fear one day.
Face it soon, decide, and move on. Time waits for no one.

To those who will never try. Why not?

Special discounts on bulk quantities of AMACOM books are
available to corporations, professional associations, and other
organizations. For details, contact Special Sales Department,
AMACOM, a division of American Management Association,
1601 Broadway, New York, NY 10019.
Tel.: 212-903-8316. Fax: 212-903-8083.
Web site: www.amacombooks.org

*This publication is designed to provide accurate and authoritative information in
regard to the subject matter covered. It is sold with the understanding that the
publisher is not engaged in rendering legal, accounting, or other professional service.
If legal advice or other expert assistance is required, the services of a competent
professional person should be sought.*

Library of Congress Cataloging-in-Publication Data

Miller, William, 1955–
     Proactive selling : control the process, win the sale / William "Skip"
Miller
          p.   cm.
     Includes bibliographical references and index.
     ISBN-10: 0-8144-0764-1
     ISBN-13: 978-0-8144-0764-6
     1. Selling—Psychological aspects.   2. Relationship marketing.   3.
Purchasing—Decision making.   I. Title.

HF5438.8.P75 M554   2002
658.85—dc21

                                                            2002014952

Printing number

10   9   8   7   6

Contents

Preface

Selling. What a profession. Why do so many people love selling so much, whereas others hate even the *thought* of selling something? What is it about the topic of selling that causes so many mixed emotions? Better yet, why are some people so good at it, and others are always trying to get it right?

> *They say successful salespeople can sell anything. They are*
>
> *right.*
>
> *They say successful salespeople are born, not made. They*
>
> *are wrong.*

Successful salespeople have five things in common:

1. They think like a customer
2. They are proactive and always think one step ahead, and therefore they pull to control the buy/sell process.
3. They have a natural curiosity. They ask. Great salespeople do not have great answers . . . they have great questions.
4. They qualify from a buyer's perspective early and often. Yes's are great, no's are great . . . maybes will kill you.
5. They use the right tool at the right time at the point of attack: the sales call.

In the years we have been doing sales and sales management training, we have observed over and over again qualities in sales professionals and the sales tools they use during a sales call that consistently set them apart from the rest of the pack. *ProActive Selling* clearly identifies the tools that successful salespeople use on a daily basis and provides them for salespeople to use so they can add value in the way they are currently selling. *ProActive Selling* is not another "sales process" book, nor is it about "strategizing a sale." There are too many books out there that define a "new way of selling" or a "new" sales methodology. A salesperson will likely get better results using his or her current, "ineffective" way than by using these books.

Believe it or not, *there is no one right way to sell.* There are many different approaches you can take to selling, and they are each very successful in their own right.

However, what is needed today is to improve the way we are selling on each and every sales call. Salespeople need to improve their sales skills and increase the number of tools they use. *ProActive Selling* provides more sales tools for the salesperson's toolbox so that at the point of attack (i.e., the sales call), a salesperson can feel he or she is fully armed, not just carrying a couple of bullets.

ProActive Selling describes what is going on in the buyer's mind and how salespeople can use this information proactively. It shows salespeople how to use the right tool at the right time so they can sell more effectively in each and every sales call.

How Salespeople Sell the Right and the Wrong Way

There is a motto for ProActive salespeople, and it is: Tactics before strategies within a process. It's that simple. Successful salespeople sell in a process. Within that process they should use tactics and then combine them with a sales strategy, rather than strategize an account and then implement tactics. It's important to put the pieces of the process in the right order, tactics before strategies, to be ProActive. Otherwise, the customer controls the sale, and the salesperson is forced into a reactive posture. Putting strategies first makes salespeople reactive. Because their tactics are poor, they are getting poor information in the development of their strategies. Putting tactics first allows the salesperson to gather quality information during a sales call so the strategy part of the sale has complete and competent information.

The number one reason salespeople lose an account is that they are out of control of the sales process. Period. That's worth saying again. The number one reason a sale is lost is because the salesperson is not in control of the buy/sell process. Salespeople will always claim the reason they won a deal is because they were *so* smart, and that the reason they lost a deal could be one of a host of other reasons, none which are in the salesperson's control, of course.

What these salespeople don't realize is that control of the buy/sell cycle is the number one factor in determining whether a sale will be won or lost, even above best fit of product or solution. In addition, this control is totally the responsibility of the salesperson. Salespeople must learn the tactics of how to control a sales process to increase their chances for success.

In discussions we have had with senior sales management, we found they all want the same things.

1. Shorter sales cycles: Shorten the sales process so more transactions can be made per salesperson.
2. Better forecasts: Better quality and quantity of deals in the pipeline—the ideal is 90 percent-plus accuracy in the 90-day forecast, rather than the 50 to 60 percent accuracy they deal with today.
3. Elimination of "maybe" or bad deals early in the cycle.
4. Control of the sale throughout the sales process, so value can be sold instead of price.
5. Lower cost of sales while increasing the average selling price (ASP) per order.
6. Implement a sales communication process into the sales organization and the rest of the company.
7. Constantly increase the competencies in the sales team to take the A players to A-plus status.

Sales managers wrestle with these strategic issues day in and day out, and must understand how easily they can be dealt with if they focus on the right things. Sales managers can have a major impact in all of the above issues if they focus on the tactics of selling and follow the rule of putting tactics before strategies; it's that straightforward. For the most part, salespeople are instructed by their managers to strategize objectively and sell to their accounts, so that the sales manager can obtain his or her own strategic objectives. It is the salesperson's job to develop and set account strategies and to deliver on them so the manager meets his or her overall objectives.

After a while, when sales are not going well, the sales manager panics a little and spends hours with a salesperson behind the scenes dabbling in account strategies that have been developed. He or she will "assist" on issues such as whom to call on, where in the organization the salesperson should call on next, and so on. He or she is "helping" to develop and refine the salesperson's account strategy of all the next strategic moves that are needed to "make the sale."

This is all good, but where are the tactics to go along with it? It's nice to work out the strategy before you get face to face with the customer, but once you are with them, what do you do? What do you say? What do you say first, second, and third? How do you end the call and stay in control? What tools do you use at the point of attack? How do make sure you control the sales call effectively, at each tactical step?

You use tactics before strategies, within a process.

ProActive Selling has 20 tools for the salesperson to use during the sales call and maintain control of the process. These tools are also the tools the sales manager can use to make sure the salesperson is really in control of the sale, at the point of attack, the sales call.

You can combine the tactics and tools of *ProActive Selling* with any of the strategic sales methodologies you like to round out your selling experience. If you have only a strategic piece of the sales puzzle, and then try to figure out the tactics to go along with it, you will falter at the point of attack. If you are armed with tactics and the buy/sell process along with your own sales strategy, you will increase your chance of success, dramatically.

The Two-Dimensional Process of Selling

Most salespeople do not have a sales process. They think they do, but try to have them describe it for you. Most salespeople can't. Without a defined sales process, salespeople can react only passively to customers. Such reactive salespeople base their approach on:

- Customer selling: The customer leads the sales process and the salesperson follows.
- Experience selling: This is the process of hoping that past experience will lead to future success.
- Catch-up selling: The competition directs the sale and then you have to play catch up all the time.
- Bad sales manager selling: The sales manager enforces the "do it like I did" methodology.
- Situational selling: The sales person is "winging it and praying" on every call.

There is a process of selling that is more successful than most so-called selling processes. It is two-dimensional; it not only has the selling process covered, but also addresses the buying process. As you will find out in Chapter 1, there is a process in how people buy. Salespeople are drilled on controlling the sales cycle, but without the added dimension of understanding the buying cycle and matching the salesperson's selling process to the buyer's buying process, they will not be in control of the overall sales process.

Traditional Tactics Are Not Enough

Salespeople are given sales tactics early on in their careers. These tactics may have included open probes/close probes, elevator speeches, and closing techniques. These are all good skills, but they are much too elementary for today's sales environment and are one-dimensional. They cannot be combined and leveraged with other skills throughout the life of a sale. Most, if not all, sales efforts today put strategies before tactics. Develop the strategic side of the sale, regardless of what the buyer wants to do, and then push the customer through a one-dimensional sales process. The heck with what the buyer wants to do; push that sales process. This can be a successful approach, but it is very reactionary and is missing the two-dimensional part of selling. It forgets about what the customer wants to do. You can argue that all the homework (strategy) a salesperson does is selling-centric. It focuses on how a salesperson plans for a sales process, regardless of the selling tactics required to accomplish the strategy and align with a buyer/seller sales cycle.

Putting tactics before strategies within a process implies that the salesperson is thinking what is needed for the next step in the *buyer*/seller relationship, and then fitting the tactics into a *buyer's* strategy, which after all is what the buyer is following. What tactics are needed to keep control of the sale and convince the buyer that he or she should follow the salesperson in an atmosphere of mutual discovery, which of course salespeople need to lead? This buying-centric nature of selling, this nonreactionary sales approach, and this buyer-first approach is the core of *ProActive Selling*, since it is all about buy/sell tactics that fit into a process.

Finally, *ProActive Selling* works even better the higher up you go in a buying organization. We all know the "trick" of calling high in a customer's organization.

Calling high is not the trick. Anyone can do that.

The trick is when you are there, what do you say?

What do you say to have the senior level executive (CEO, CIO, CFO, COO, etc.) treat the salesperson as a value-add asset and to have the executive stay engaged? How can you avoid the C-level executive sending you down into the bowels of the organization from which it is nearly impossible to get back up? *ProActive Selling* addresses not only what salespeople have to say at the CXO (Chief X-*fill in the blank* Officer) level, but gets them comfortable in calling high and staying high, as well as being a value-add to the senior level executive. *ProActive Selling* is so good at the CXO level that salespeople typically find the senior executives of the account calling them and asking the salesperson what they should do next.

Tactics before strategies in a two-dimensional selling model is what *ProActive Selling* is all about. It is what makes successful salespeople great. It is their attitude of:

- Focusing on how people buy, not how they should sell.
- Focusing on the buy/sell process, not just the sales process.
- Looking at the sale as a series of buyer-related steps
- Qualifying early in the process and then deciding if the salesperson wants to spend time with an account, rather than hoping the buyer wants to spend time with them.
- Taking control and having the buyer follow the salesperson's lead.
- Closing at the beginning of the process, not at the end. There is no such thing as a great closer, or "great closing skills."
- Having the right tools at the right time for the right call.

By successfully reading and implementing the tactics and processes in *ProActive Selling*, salespeople will be able to:

- Accomplish more in less time.
- Be proactive and anticipate the next sales step.
- Motivate themselves to call successfully at all levels in the organization.
- Control the sales process. The salesperson who controls the sales process . . . wins.
- Get rid of maybes in their sales funnel.
- Learn where to hunt and use their time most effectively.
- Plan and utilize homework on the sales call.
- Lower the overall cost of sales.
- Increase the average selling price per order.
- Create a powerful sales introduction on every sales call.
- End every sales call and stay in complete control of the sale.
- Understand the buyer's motivational direction.

- Master the seven qualification questions to call on the right accounts all the time.
- Speak the right language to the right level of buyer.
- Change a maybe to a decision easily and effectively.

On a final note, we use the term *prospect* in this book rather freely. When we say prospect, we mean an individual or a group of individuals who are chartered to make a purchase decision. It could be anyone from an individual buying a new computer to a major corporation working through a committee to make a decision on a new infrastructure automation system. There are many differences at the strategic level between these examples, but the buy process and the tools a salesperson uses during the sales call are easily transferable.

For the most part, selling is selling, so *ProActive Selling* works if you are selling a product, service, or tangible or intangible item. It works when selling over the phone, over the Internet, face to face, or through channels. The examples in the book are simple and easy, but it should not be misconstrued that *ProActive Selling* is effective only for simple sales situations. The *strategies* of a sale can and do change based on what you are selling, usually based on the size of the order and length of the sale cycle. The tactics and process of a sale rarely change, regardless of the sale size or length of a sale, since it all involves sales calls, which is what *ProActive Selling* is here to make you better at. Good luck, and learn how to better your sales skills. . . . ProActively.

Acknowledgments

To the customers of M3 Learning and users of ProActive Selling—thanks for believing and using ProActive Selling. You constantly tell us how well it works.

To my friends and family—thanks for your valued insight and opinions. ProActive Selling would not be around without you.

To my mom and dad—you did it right.

Chapter 1

ProActive Selling: Having the Right Tools at the Right Time to Be a Step Ahead

It was the end of an important meeting. Brad had spent weeks getting this meeting together so he and his company could be included in the client company's evaluation. He had just made a presentation to the customer's senior management team and was very pleased with how it went.

> *"Brad, this looks very, very interesting to us," the senior vice president said, "and we like what we see. Why don't you call on Kurt and Seline, who are heading up this selection, and start working with them? They have been at this for a few weeks, and you should be considered along with the other people we are looking at right now."*

Brad is certainly excited. He is happy with the way the presentation went, and the senior vice president is now telling him what he should do next. This follows the old sales rule that if you just do what the prospect tells you to do, and you do it well, then the order will follow. Right? Wrong!

If Brad does what the senior vice president wants him to do, he loses control of the sale, which puts him at a disadvantage. Remember the Law of Sales Control.

THE LAW OF SALES CONTROL

The buyer is *always* neutral. If you are not in control of the sale, and the buyer is neutral, then someone else is in control, and it is usually the competition. (And that competition could be an alternate choice of action, such as to do nothing, spend the money elsewhere, or delay the process, or a competitor. Anything that prevents you from getting an order is competition.)

Brad needs to use the Summarize, Bridge, and Pull^{Tool} to stay in control of this meeting. He has to identify the next step and have the customer agree to it, not just do what the senior vice president tells him to do. Senior executives want to be guided just like lower level people in the buyer's organization. They just give you very little time to take control, since they are used to having it. They will give up control, however, if you have a planned-out next step that makes sense to them and is seen as helpful to them.

"Mr. Henry, that is a very good idea to bring Kurt and Seline into this process. It sounds like we have had a good meeting today. You have stated your desire to increase capacity by 10 percent in your current channels while keeping costs constant. You have also stated you want to have a solution in place by the end of the year. We have brought to light some solutions that may be very appealing, so I think we have had a good meeting today, would you agree?"

"Yes, I would say so."

"Great. A good next step then would be for us to get together with Kurt and Seline to really dig into the business issues that are driving you right now on this decision, as well as to get together with you and discuss the overall risks to you and the business strategy. You will then be in a good position from a technical as well as a financial perspective to make a decision if you should continue to go forward with this process. Does this sound like a good next step to you?"

By using a tool we will learn in Chapter 3, *Summarize, Bridge, and Pull*, Brad stayed in control of this sale. He has now been ProActive, not reactive, and has increased his chances of getting this sale.

Tool-Based ProActive Selling

What happened here? What went on during this sales call? Isn't it common for a salesperson to get excited during a sale when the customer gives direction on what to do next, especially if it is a senior manager? All too often, the best sales strategy is planned out before the call, and then during the sales call, the salesperson makes a mistake and loses control. If Brad does what the senior executive asked him to do, that is, talk to Kurt and Seline, Brad will be spending much more time adjusting the sales strategy with his sales manager than building his selling tactics around the new strategy. He will be in a reactive sales mode and will be hoping that the customer selects him and his company as the winning vendor. He will also be hoping to see the senior manager again at some time during the process. Hope is a good thing, but not in sales. Putting strategies in front of tactics results in merely hoping for a good outcome, and is the wrong approach.

Instead of just hoping for the best, salespeople need to develop a toolbox of selling tools, so that when they make their pitch, they can execute their sales tactics flawlessly. The strategy part of selling comes later.

Brad used his *Summarize, Bridge, and Pull* tool, a tactic to keep the buy/sell process under his control. By mastering his sales tools, Brad was able to keep this deal alive and own the buy/sell process.

When all is said and done, the salesperson who owns the process owns the deal. Keeping in control of the process is the hard part, especially if you do not have the tools to do the job correctly. *ProActive Selling* has 20 sales tools and five sales manager tools that you can use during the sales call to establish, recover from, and maintain control of the sales process. These will help you to increase the chances a deal will go your way and minimize the chances you will hear a no, or worse, a maybe.

The Customer's Perspective

Successful salespeople understand the buyer's as well as the seller's perspective. They understand that the most critical element in a sale is the prospect, since the prospect is the one who is placing the order, will be using the product/service, and will be paying for it. Top salespeople know that the buyer's perspective is much more important than theirs. Otherwise, their sales message will be loaded down with information the buyer is not interested in. An example of poorly constructed sales messages are those that center around the "value proposition."

> *"It is very important for us right now to succeed. For us*
>
> *to make that happen, the customer needs to understand our*
>
> *new value proposition."*
>
> *"We have to be extremely clear in our value proposition to*
>
> *our potential clients."*

"We have to lead with our value statements, then get into

the rest of the presentation."

Have you ever heard anything so one sided? The truth is, the prospect could *care less* about your value proposition. What they care about is *their* value proposition—the value *they* are supplying to *their* customers.

If you take the perspective of the customers in the value proposition theory, you will find out how your product or service will help make them money and help them become more competitive. The real value proposition is taking the prospect's perspective as well as yours.

What Is a Buy/Sell Process?

As you read this book, you will find that the *buy/sell* sales process is different from what you may be used to, since you will be thinking like a buyer as well as a seller.

Just for a moment though, forget about how you should sell. Forget about selling methodologies, selling processes, or how you go through a sales cycle. Instead, think like a buyer.

A little reflection shows there is a process in how people buy. If you can define that process, you can understand where a prospect is headed and what steps he is taking to get there. Because you know where he is going, you can then be a step ahead and pull the prospect through their buying process. You can control the prospect's buying process. You do not have to guess at all.

If you understand the process of how a prospect buys, you can be ProActive. You can be a step ahead and pull the prospect to the next step along the way—pulling, not pushing, the sale. When you pull, you are in control. When you push, someone else is in control. (Remember, no one likes a pushy salesperson.)

A prospect goes through a number of different phases in a buying process, each with its own unique set of requirements.

Initial Interest

The first phase in the buying process is for prospects to have an *Initial Interest.*

People can be interested in many things.

"I'm interested in buying a new car."

"I'm interested in a new TV."

"I need to buy a new machine for the factory floor."

"I am interested in looking at a consulting service right now."

"I need an answer to a current problem I have."

Although important, interests are not enough for the buyer to make a purchase or actually to do something. It's when the prospect is motivated to do something about that interest that she starts a buying process. Motivation is the difference between being interested and needing or desiring something; it has motion, and it starts to have a life of its own. *Initial Interest* is more than just interest; it is motivation driving a need or desire.

A motivated prospect will start some action, but how can you motivate a prospect? How motivated is the prospect to begin with? How can you get a prospect to see she has a need for what your product or service can do for her?

Salespeople use several techniques to motivate their clients to buy:

- Find the pain.
- Press their hot button.
- Instill fear, uncertainty, and doubt (FUD factor).
- Appeal to value and Return on Investment (ROI).
- Identify the real need.
- Have them understand the value proposition.

It's hard to argue with these techniques, but they don't adequately respond to a buyer's motivation.

There are two motivators that affect human behavior: pain and pleasure. Therefore most people orient their behavior around the avoidance of pain or the obtainment of pleasure.

In sales, you are really not interested in motivation per se, since by itself, without a need, motivation is stagnant and has no time definition or motion, two critical elements of selling. So motivation with a need is still not very useful to a salesperson without a time and motion element. What *is* useful to a salesperson is motivational direction. Motivational direction directly addresses the pain/pleasure motivation of a prospect. It covers the avoidance part of pain, which we will call AWAY, and the attainment part of pleasure, which we will call TOWARDS. TOWARDS and AWAY are what salespeople are really interested in during the *Initial Interest* part of the buy process.

Tool TOWARDS/AWAY Tool

Prospects are either "TOWARDS buyers" or "AWAY buyers." For the most part, this is absolute. They tend either to move away from pain or towards pleasure, and how they are motivated affects their buying patterns. How do you find out whether someone is a TOWARDS or AWAY buyer? Listen to what they tell you.

AWAY buyers will always have that negative spin. They will tell you what motivates them is the avoidance of something. When asked a question like, "Why would you buy a new TV?" AWAY buyers would respond:

- The old one just isn't working right.
- It doesn't have the features on it I need.
- I can't get the channels I want.
- My old one is pretty well shot.
- I am tired of looking at such a small screen.

All focused on the negative part of the sale. AWAY people are moving away from something, usually away from some sort of pain.

The prospect who is a TOWARDS buyer would have a very different reaction to the same question.

- I like the new features.
- I like the looks of it.
- It will fit great in my entertainment center.
- I want to watch my movies on a big screen.
- I want to feel the action in my living room.

There's nothing negative about their responses. Instead, they identify all positive, forward moving reasons, and this marks the characteristics of a TOWARDS buyer. They don't express any thoughts on the previous product, but rather focus on the desirable features of the new one.

There is one other type of buyer who tries to evade the question. When asked, "Why would you want a new TV?" these buyers respond with comments like:

- I just want one.
- I need one.
- I don't know, I just need one.

For these types of buyers, you need to ask again gently, "Why would you really buy one? When it comes down to it, why would you buy a new TV?" They usually then really search their feelings and tell you their reasons. Nine times out of ten, they will give you an AWAY reason. These people are really saying:

"I am an AWAY buyer. Don't tell me how great something is,

or how much more use I will get out of something, because I

do not care! I will agree with your logic, but it will not moti-

vate me. Tell me what I can't have, won't get, or will lose by

not having your product, and you have my attention."

Many years ago, I had an old Mercedes Benz. It was well over 10 years old, and I was thinking about getting a new car. People would come up and tell me about new features certain cars had, and how one car had a new this or a new that, and I really agreed with their logic. Even so, I was not motivated to do anything about it.

Then one day, my brother came up to me and said I needed a new car. I assured him I was looking but had not seen a reason to buy something else than what I already had. His comment to me was that I should not care about those other reasons either.

The reason he offered for why I should buy a new car was that the car I owned was starting to look old, and quite frankly, I was starting to look old in that old car.

Me?! Looking old? In my car?!

I started to drive past retail store windows and to see if in fact the car was starting to look old, or if I was starting to look old in the car. It didn't matter what I thought; the damage was done. I didn't want to start looking old in an old car! Within 30 days, I bought a new car.

Psychologically, 70 percent of the world's population is AWAY. One hundred percent of your company's sales literature is TOWARDS. It's no wonder that the TOWARDS sales literature that pronounces the latest and greatest features and functions about your product or service quickly becomes trash basket fodder for senior salespeople. If sales and marketing people tell customers what they won't get, can't have, can avoid doing, they will get the attention of 70 percent of the audience.

Sales Literature Direction Words

TOWARDS	AWAY
Great	Stop
New	Avoid
Improve	Less
40 Percent better	Before it is too late
Act now	Prevent

Sales materials should also emphasize the pleasure of buying the product (TOWARDS). Thirty percent of the buyers are TOWARDS, and they have no concept of "finding the pain."

They have a vision, a mission, a path they are on, and they need those TOWARDS reasons. You want to be able to sell to both types of the buyers' motivational directions.

Buyers are interested in many things. Based on how they prioritize and are motivated over time, their motivational direction to do something about it will determine whether their interest level is high enough for them to continue their movement and to go to the next phase called *Educate.*

Educate

If they are motivated past the *Initial Interest* phase, buyers will want to educate themselves more on what they can do to satisfy an initial need they have developed. Salespeople usually have this part down, using Feature/Benefit or Feature/Advantage/Benefit selling techniques. Buyers want more information and they get it through a variety of sources. Take, for example, someone who is interested in buying a car. Once past the point of *Initial Interest,* she now wants to gather information about the car. She can read some information about it, listen to someone who has some knowledge of cars or a particular car she is interested in, read about information through advertising, or physically go to a car dealer and see it. There are a variety of ways buyers can get information that they need.

If the buyer's interest wanes at this point, if the information she obtains during this phase does not keep her level of motivation high, then the buyer will stop the buying process. The potential purchase will become a secondary or tertiary priority and go back into that *Initial Interest* area with the buyer now having a lower degree of motivation. There will be little or no interest to do anything about it. If, however, the buyer is still interested and is still motivated, she will continue up the buying path. She will stick to her process and go to the next phase, called *Transfer of Ownership.*

Transfer of Ownership

Now comes the most interesting part of the buyer's process. Here the buyer either gets on board or stops the buying evaluation. This is where the buyer takes ownership of the solution being offered, decides to stay in the education mode, or stops the evaluation all together. Welcome to *Transfer of Ownership.*

All salespersons know when transfer of ownership takes place because they have been in sales situations in which the buyer "gets it." The buyer now understands how he would be able to use the product or service being offered and agrees with the benefits—what's in it for me (WIIFM).

> *Every salesperson has experienced this feeling of transfer of ownership. This moment when the prospect says, "OK, I get it now. If I buy this service/product and implement it this way, then I will be able to do this and that, and then I will really start saving money on . . ."*

The customers start selling themselves. It is what every salesperson dreams will happen on every sales call. The prospect gets it and now is pushing you on how fast something can be done. The pressure is now on the salesperson to follow through.

Transfer of ownership must occur for a prospect to continue on in their buying process. It happens in one of two ways. Either the prospects take ownership of the product/service themselves, or they are induced into taking ownership. Either they figure it out on their own, or the salesperson has helped them figure it out. The first way is reactive. The prospect is reacting to information, and then on his or her own finally gets it. The second way is ProActive. The salesperson has helped lead the buyer through the *Transfer of Ownership* stage. He or she has *proactively induced* the transfer of ownership in the buyer's mind. If transfer of ownership happens through the first way, the salesperson was simply lucky. If it happens through the second way, the salesperson was good.

THE LAW OF BEING LUCKY RATHER THAN GOOD

"I'd rather be lucky than good" . . . nah . . . I'd rather be good, because it is repeatable and leveragable. I can recreate success over and over again.

Be a good salesperson so you can be proactive in the right situation at the right time again and again and again. How do salespeople proactively induce transfer of ownership?

As a first example, let's say you are interested in buying a pair of shoes. Either your old ones are getting pretty bad (AWAY), or there are some new ones you really desire (TO-WARDS). Whatever the motivation direction may be, you have an interest in a pair of shoes. The interest is so high that you take time to educate yourself on shoes. You may look in a catalog, a fashion magazine, or at other people's feet; you may actually go down to the store and window shop. If your motivation is still high at this point, and you see a pair that may be of some interest to you, you pick up the display sample, find a salesperson, and say, "Can I please see these in a size X?"

Now the store clerk goes away for a few minutes, and comes back with the pair of shoes you want to try on. Then you make a decision, yes or no, on this particular pair of shoes. This is a typical shoe selling experience. If the salesperson was ProActive, he came back with not just the pair you asked to see, but with two or three additional pairs of shoes for you to try on. Why would a salesperson take so much time in the back room, risk losing you because you don't like to wait, to bring you out a pair of shoes you have requested, and two or three pairs you did not request?

Good salespeople know their job is not to sell you shoes; it is to get you to try them on. They know once you have a pair of shoes on your feet, they have a better chance at a sale than if you did not take some physical action and get involved. Good shoe salespeople are not wasting time; they are just trying to increase their odds at getting a sale. Good shoe sales people are ProActive and can proactively induce the transfer of ownership.

As a second example, a software company has just given an hour demonstration to a client. The demonstration was set up to transfer ownership, not just to educate. The salesperson is a ProActive one. The meeting is about to adjourn. All she has to do is give a final closing summary, have the software engineer say a few final words, and then propose a next step. You might think that the demonstration, or transfer of ownership in this case, was the 45 minutes or so the software engineer had the customers in front of the computer screen. They asked some questions, the salesperson answered them, and things looked good. They seemed really to understand the software. The salesperson might make the mistake of offering as the next step a proposal to keep this sale moving. Instead, now is the perfect time to complete the transfer of ownership. The salesperson, before the final summary and proposal to go to the next step, stops and turns to the customer and says,

"Based on what you have seen today, let's assume you had

a system like this successfully up and running for 6

months now. What decisions would you be making now?

What other decisions would you be making knowing you

had the right information this system provides?"

The conversation is now completing the transfer of ownership in the clients' minds. The salesperson is using a Time Demo^{Tool}, which is a transfer of ownership tool described in Chapter 7. Instead of the salesperson pushing, the clients are talking about how the system will solve their problems. They are thinking about how they could make decisions on important business issues they cannot make now since they do not have this type of information available to them.

Transfer of ownership is the step most salespeople skip. They very incorrectly assume it is part of the education step. You will find out in Chapter 7 how *Transfer of Ownership* happens and how to master this step.

Rationalize

Once the buyer has completed the transfer of ownership, a unique thing happens. He starts to think,

"Is this the right time to make a decision like this?"

"Have we looked at enough options?"

"Is this the right tool for us or should we look at a few more?"

Salespeople have names for things that happen when buyers enter into the *Rationalize* phase, such as objections, cold feet, buyer's remorse, final objections, stuck at the final step, and maybeland.

Salespeople do not anticipate the buyer having to go through a final rationalization process. But buyers do. After a great demonstration, salespeople are eager to put together a final proposal, get it approved, and have the customer sign it ASAP. Reactive salespeople think like this because this is how salespeople generally have been taught to think. However, it is not how a buyer, or a ProActive sales person for that matter, thinks.

After completing a transfer of ownership and proceeding up the decision path, buyers need one more final justification, one more rationalization. This happens all the time. You try the shoes on one more time. You are ready to buy the shoes, but want to try both on, just to be sure. You are ready to buy the car, but want to look at it one more time before the salesperson comes back with the final papers. Executives call a final meeting with the people who are in charge of using the product or service to make sure, one more time, "we are doing the right thing" by investing the company's resources and the executive team's reputation. You want to sleep on a decision overnight just to straighten out your thoughts. This is the buyer's final justification experience, or their final rationalization.

Sometimes the buyer breezes through this phase; sometimes it takes a long time and can most definitely kill a deal if it "hangs" in this stage too long without progress. It seems the larger the sale, the more time a buyer spends in this stage. However, buyers who stay in the Rationalization phase too long tend to see the proposed solution now as too old or not current, or, after having slept on it, still cannot make a decision, so was it really right the first time? Buyers need to rationalize a purchase before they make a final decision. The ProActive salesperson is aware of this step and uses ProActive tools to stay in control of the sale.

Decide

The actual decision is the final buying step. If a buyer has gone through the buying cycle and is still motivated, she will make a decision. It will be either yes or no. It is that simple. The buyer decides yes or no, not "Should I sign this order today?" so our definition of *close* is not the reactive "getting an order." Getting an order is a "selling" mentality. Buyers dislike being "sold to."

Our definition of close is obtaining a decision, either yes or no, without delay. Yes's are great, no's are great (for different reasons); it's the maybes that will kill you. Time is the enemy here, and here is where most salespeople make the biggest mistake.

> *"I just need to polish up my closing skills."*
>
> *"I can sell. I just need to add a few more closing skills in*
>
> *my repertoire."*
>
> *"I do everything right, then things fall apart at the close."*
>
> *"My boss says I am just afraid to ask for the order, but I am*
>
> *asking for the order. It's just not coming in yet."*

As you will find out in Chapter 8, there are really no good "closing skills." There are some negotiating skills you can use in this or any step of selling, but if you are looking for those great closing skills, or even great "trial" closing skills, you will not find them here. Buyers don't "close." They make decisions based on the buying process that has just been described. So the skills you will learn about in *Close* will be focused on having the buyer feel like the close of a deal is just the final step in a natural buying process. There are no high-pressure (money losing) tactics here, just some tools to help the buyer through the final step of his buying process.

Matching the Sell Process to the Buy Process

Throughout *ProActive Selling*, you will use the buy process, match it to the sell process, and see how you can always be in control of the sale. Own the process; own the deal.

The Buy/Sell Process is described in Figure 1.1. A buyer's process and a seller's process are similar, but with different perspectives. A buyer goes through

- Initial Interest
- Education
- Transfer of Ownership
- Rationalization
- Decide

A seller goes through a similar, parallel process.

- Initial Interest = Initiate
- Education = Educate
- Transfer of Ownership = Validate
- Rationalize = Justify
- Decide = Close

Since this book is for selling purposes, we will call the phases by their selling names, but the buying names are just as applicable.

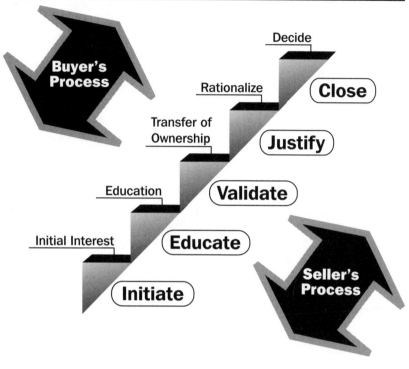

Figure 1-1. The Buy/Sell Process

If you own the process, you own the deal and win the sale. It is very true that people buy from people they like and trust. It's important to improve rapport building and communication skills so that you convey trustworthiness, but it is more important to concentrate on leading the process so that you will own the deal.

Think like a buyer and match your sales process to the buyer's buying process. If you are ProActive and really work the sale from the buyer's perspective, you take the guesswork out of the equation. You know where the buyer is going. You know the buying steps he will be taking, and you don't have to wait for the buyer to "make up his mind" during the sale. You know where he is going and can suggest the next step he should take. If you work a sale this way, you are a ProActive salesperson who will be in control and a step ahead—always.

The Length of a Sales Cycle

Before you get into the buy/sell process and the ProActive tools, a word needs to be said on the length of a sale. Some sales cycles are days in duration. Some are completed in minutes. Most sales are measured in weeks and months. What seems to be the gating factor in determining the length of a sale cycle are investment, risk, and sales competencies. Investment and risk are issues determined by both the buyer and the seller. Sales competencies, however, stem from the salesperson and are therefore an area salespeople have in their control.

If the investment and risk of a decision are low to the buyer and to his organization, he will tend to hurry up the process. If the investment and risk are high, buyers tend to take a longer time, since more people and departments are usually involved in the purchase. Risk and investment are not inseparable. If risk is high and the investment is low, a decision can still take a long time. This is also true when the investment is high and the risk low. Selling organizations balance investment and risk decisions all the time as well to determine whether the reward of the sales is worth the risk and time investment.

Sales competencies are something the salesperson and sales organization have control over, so the ability to affect the desired outcome, shorter sales cycles, can be realized to a large extent by improvement in selling competencies.

On the average, buy/sell cycles are 20 to 30 percent longer than they need to be. If a sales cycle is typically 3 to 4 months in your organization, you should be able to eliminate 20 to 30 percent of this time estimate. How can you be sure of this?

- Good salespeople are already doing this.
- With control of the buy/sell process, the delays and slips go away.

- Since you are in control, the competition is at a disadvantage and is marching to your time schedule. (You know this to be true since you have been on the other side of this phenomenon.)
- Transfer of ownership has been completed and is anchored to your solution.
- The buyer has seen the value and knows that delaying is costing him or her a lot.

You can shorten your sales cycles by increasing sales competencies that control the process. You need to control the buy/sell process tactically, within the process, and then update and implement your sales strategy. It is these tactics, these ProActive tools that you will be using within the buy/sell process, that will make you a ProActive salesperson.

Why Follow a Process?

You follow a process because it's all about direction. The buyer is progressing through a process, and you can choose to lead, follow, or get out of the way. Buyers need direction with their process. You can provide this direction and add value to their process, especially at the higher levels within an organization.

If you have confidence in the process and the ability to lead and provide direction, buyers will follow you. You will be in charge, you will have a plan and a process, and the confidence you project is contagious. Without a process, the buyers are left to their own devices, and as we discussed before, a buyer is always neutral. They want to be led, and led down a process. Make it your process, which mirrors the buy process so as to feel very natural for a buyer.

Mastering the buy/sell process will shorten your sales cycles, provide you with control, and give you direction throughout the sale. Without it, a salesperson is at the whim of the buyer, or worse, the competition. Learning and practicing the buy/sell process, and applying the ProActive tools you are about to learn, will result in a fully armed and competent salesperson.

Chapter 2

Do Your Homework
Before the Sale

In the homework part of the sale, the salesperson becomes familiar with the account and the industry before she starts selling to it. Many sales strategy books are available that are very good at plotting out the homework needed for major accounts. *ProActive Selling* does not want to make any substitutions in the sales strategy you may be using now. Rather, if you currently have a sales Initiate process, you will be augmenting it with a few more tools. If you do not have a sales strategy homework process, use this one.

The homework a salesperson gathers before the sale actually begins is as critical as in any profession, whether it is an Indy car driver checking out his race car before the race, a musician tuning her instrument before the concert, or a surgeon checking over his operating room instruments before the operation. The amount and specific type of homework a salesperson does is key to success. For sales, the amount of homework should vary based on the size of the opportunity and the overall importance of the account. You will do more homework on a large potential account than you will for a very small opportunity. A company with annual sales of $250,000,000 would probably get more attention from you than an account with $250,000 in annual revenue. This may not be true in all cases, but later in this chapter you will see how to quantify an opportunity.

For you, homework is the amount of work needed to get enough information on the account to discuss intelligently the business issues that are important to the customer. It may take 5 minutes or 5 hours per account. It can be as easy as checking out a Web site to doing some deep financial investigation. Homework should be a process, and in that process, we should seek to answer five questions:

1. Where should I spend my sales time wisely?
2. What accounts should I call on?
3. When should I focus my time on selling?
4. How should I organize myself to be effective during selling time?
5. Who should I actually call on, and what should I say to them?

Where Should You Spend Your Sales Time?

Salespeople love to sell and to do whatever selling activities it takes to make a sale. They are under the impression that if they do a lot of sales activities, whatever they may be, they will make sales and earn a lot of money. You can hear it in their voices.

"All I have to do is a lot of sales activities. If I do them these as fast and as well as I can, I will be successful."

"If I just send out 10 proposals per week, the numbers will work in my favor."

"Twenty five prospecting letters per week is all I have to do to get someone to call me back."

Bzzz. Thanks for playing, but these are the wrong answers. The law of sales activities states:

The Law of Sales Activities

It's not just the amount of activities that makes a salesperson successful. It is doing a lot of the right activities, at the right place, at the right time, and delivered to the right audience.

So of course, you want to define what right is. Start with the right place. Where should you spend your time wisely?

Tool **The ProActive Sales Matrix**Tool

In *ProActive Sales Management,* we defined the ProActive Sales Matrix for managers. We advised managers on where they should spend their time. The same concept applies for salespeople because both need to strategize with the same sales vocabulary.

Salespeople need to prospect, even though it is not at the top of the list of things they want to do on a day-by-day basis. Most salespeople need to prioritize their selling time, and they do a poor job at it. A method of prospecting commonly used by salespeople is the reactive A/B/C method, in which a salesperson takes what he has in his sales funnel and assigns the following rankings:

A: My best, my top, my biggest, the soonest to close accounts

B: The ones I am working on—analogous to work in process inventory

C: The ones that I am just starting on, that it is way too early to tell about (also known as the list I generate 2 days before my account review with my boss to show him that I am working.)

This is an attempt at prioritizing accounts so a salesperson can be effective, but it is one-dimensional. It takes a single picture in time, but does not take the future into account. It does not tell anyone what the salesperson should be doing, or where he should be spending his time. It is also too qualitative; there are no quantitative measurements.

For example, which is an *A* deal for a salesperson who has a typical order size of $50,000?

> **1.** One that is going to close in 2 weeks, but for $15,000?
> **2.** One that is going to close in 4 months, but is worth $125,000?
> **3.** One that is going to be worth $250,000, but will take 9 months to close, and you really haven't started to call on them yet?
> **4.** One that is worth $40,000 for a current account?
> **5.** One that is worth $30,000 from a new name competitive win account?
> **6.** All of the above?
> **7.** None of the above?

The A/B/C method is a little too subjective, and it allows salespeople wiggle room so they can "lie to themselves." Where there is a plethora of subjectivity and a lack of objectivity, salespeople typically would rather make the numbers look like they want them to look (lie to themselves), rather than look at the numbers as they really are. Instead, you need to put a little objectivity into the subjective process of sales territory planning. You add objectivity by adding another quantitative dimension.

Being ProActive: Adding a Second Dimension

To be ProActive, salespeople need to be definitive on what they want to do. They must be quantitative. They must stick to a process that lets them see reality, rather than the rose-colored version of reality. To do this, you need to add a second dimension to the sales forecasting process.

Instead of just forecasting with an A/B/C system, add another element: time. Time will give you a two-dimensional system of forecasting.

Old Way   *New Way*

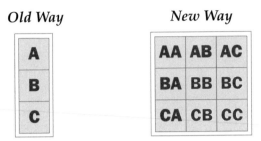

The Old Way

The old way is one dimensional, and the A/B/C values can mean anything a salesperson wants them to mean. The A/B/C values can stand for how important an account is, how much it is worth, how soon it is going to close, how qualified an account is, and so on. This is not a very effective way of determining where you should be spending your time, since you are not measuring time.

The New Way

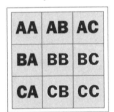

For the New Way, you add a second digit. By adding this second digit or time element to the matrix, you now have a two-dimensional representation of where you should be spending your time, since you are quantifying time. The digits represent time, and the letters themselves stand for a value.

The Digits

The first digit (nonbolded) signifies *the length of time.* It can represent either

1. Last 12 months of business or
2. Potential size of a customer in 12 months.

In most cases, you will be sizing up the last 12 months of business this customer has done with you as the key metric.

If you are a start-up business, a new division, or entering a new market, you may not have any history to measure your accounts with any degree of realism. Use the second metric, the potential size of a customer in the next 12 months metric then. For now though, assume the typical business case, and use the last 12 months of business the customer has done with you.

The second digit (bolded) signifies *deal forecast time.* It identifies what the customer will do with you in an x timeframe, where x = a typical timeframe it takes to close a forecasted deal. It is usually a 90-day window, but some industries are measured in days or weeks; others use 6 to 9 months. Typical is a one-quarter or a 90-day view of future potential.

The Letter Values

Here is where the letters come in. You need to assign a quantitative value to the letters. Again they will vary by industry, company, division, sales team, and even by individual salesperson. Once they are assigned, the quantitative part of the ProActive Sales Matrix kicks in.

Let's assign the quantitative measurement, dollars, to the letters in an example.

A = ≥ $100,000
B = $20,000–$100,000
C = ≤ $20,000

An *A* is a deal in excess of $100,000. It is a quantified number and there is no subjectivity about it. It cannot be just a major account, one that you have been working a long time or one that is of strategic value. It is what it is, a prospect that has a value greater than $100,000.

When you now combine these two dimensions together, you arrive at the ProActive Sales Matrix.

AA	AB	AC
BA	BB	BC
CA	CB	CC

If you now apply the digit and letter nomenclature together, you understand the matrix. So in this example,

- An *AA* deal is one in which the customer has done more than $100,000 of business with you over the last 12 months, and can potentially spend more than $100,000 in the next 90 days. (Another example, for salespeople who do not have a lot of repeat business, is to say this is an account that is in the top 10 percent of the clients we want to do business with, and in the next 90 days, they will spend over $100,000 with us. Use the matrix to fit your situation.)
- A *BC* deal is one in which the customer has spent between $20,000 and $100,000 with you in the past year (or is medium size potential), but in the next 90 days, has the potential to spend very little with you, less than $20,000.
- An *AC* account is one in which in the last 12 months, the customer has spent a lot of money with you (*A*), but in the next 90 days, plans on spending little or no money with you (*C*).

The ProActive Sales Matrix is a planning tool ProActive salespeople need to live by. You have your organizer, your Palm, your Day timer, as well as Microsoft Explorer and Outlook doing a great deal of "scheduling" for you. How are you at being ProActive and using a scheduler for your benefit, rather than having it use you? Your organizer tells you what you have scheduled, not what you should be scheduling. The ProActive Sales Matrix tells you what you should be doing and where you should be spending your time. But there's more. There are three zones in the ProActive Matrix.

The Dead Zone

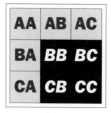

The Dead Zone is where salespeople who are reactive typically spend 60 to 80 percent of their time, responding to customer requests. These are the customers who are always calling you. They have a question, an issue, want another quote, do not understand a point, need another demo . . . you get the point.

These customers are truly important, but you are spending too much time here. There are actually some customers in this zone you wish would consider going to the competition! You need to spend a lot less time in the Dead Zone.

The Maintain Zone

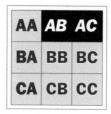

In the Maintain Zone, salespeople are doing exactly what they need to do with these accounts: maintain and try to grow business. These are important accounts, and salespeople need to keep relationships here in good standing. They need to spend time being ProActive and looking for additional business with these accounts as well as maintaining the current relationship. Salespeople typically allocate 10 to 30 percent of their time in this zone, which is the right amount of time to spend with these accounts.

The RedZone

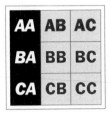

The RedZone is where the action is. This is where the key, large deals are going to happen. Salespeople are typically calling on the *AA* potentials because they know these customers and they have an idea of what they are doing, since these prospects have made a major purchase within the last 12 months. However, if salespeople are spending 60 to 80 percent of their time in the Dead Zone, and 10 to 30 percent of their time in the Maintain Zone, how much time are they spending in the rest of the Red-Zone? Not enough? That's right.

What should salespeople do about it? As noted photographer DeWitt Jones puts it, "To be great, you need to be in the area of most potential." To be great in sales, you need to spend more time in the sales area of most potential: the RedZone.

Why ProActive Scheduling?

You know the rules now. You need to be ProActive with your schedule and get control of it. Why? The real question is why salespeople spend the time that they do in these three zones.

Salespeople are chartered to do sales activities, believing that if they do enough of these, they will get enough sales.

> "OK, between 8:00 A.M. and 5:00 P.M., if I do enough sales
>
> activities, if I am selling or talking to prospects/customers
>
> during this time, then I will make my quota for the year.
>
> More things going on means more sales."

This is a very reactive statement. Salespeople try to avoid or, at best, manage risk. Some risk is good, but typically, if one can avoid risk, or at least manage it, one has a higher probability of success. Why take unnecessary risks if you can avoid it, right?

For a salesperson to spend time in the Dead Zone, how much risk does he have to take on? These Dead Zone prospects are calling him, and the only sales activity a salesperson needs to do is *return* the prospect's call.

"Hi, this is Eric Mowbrey. Is Mr. Carson in?"

"May I tell him what this is in regards to?"

"I'm returning his call."

"Oh, I'll put you right through."

They are calling you, so you have the right to talk to them. The personal risk to the salesperson is low, but the potential return is also low. A low-risk, low-return situation is not a good place in which to be spending quality sales time.

Salespeople do need to spend some time in the Maintain Zone. These are the accounts that have purchased a lot from you recently and will purchase something from you in the near future. It may not be much this particular time, but these are important accounts to mind.

Because these people are important to you, you end up spending time with them. They are not calling you, but they know and trust you. You have a business relationship with these people, and they are under a basic business courtesy rule to maintain a relationship with you. You have worked with them before, and if you call Maintain Zone customers, they will at least *take* the call.

"Hi, is Mr. Carson in?"

"May I tell him who is calling?"

"This is Eric Mowbrey."

"With what company?"

"Oh, he knows me."

Again, the risk here is still low. It is higher than that of the Dead Zone call, but still low since you are calling a "friend" or business acquaintance. This is therefore a low-risk, low-reward call.

Now comes the RedZone. Outside of the *AA* deals, since you already have a relationship with these accounts, and if a big deal is going on, you are probably spending some time with them, you need to take some risks in the RedZone and start *prospecting.* It is a risky proposition, but it *is* the area of most potential. Like in American football, the RedZone is where you are going to score most of your points (the area from the opposing team's 20-yard line to their goal line). The odds are in your favor. The expectation to win in the RedZone is high, which is why most salespeople avoid it. High risk could mean Big Loss, and salespeople hate to lose. They have a fear of losing. You want to be in the RedZone and have tools in your toolbox ready to make you successful and lower your risk as well as your fears.

Most salespeople have a real aversion to prospecting. It is something that has to be done, but most salespeople would rather do *anything* else than to prospect all day long.

THE LAW OF THE REACTIVE SALESPERSON'S PROSPECTING MOTTO

"OK, it's 8:00 A.M. Should I start prospecting, or should I poke myself in the eye with a pencil? Either choice is bad, but at least when I poke myself in the eye, I can go to the doctor and avoid prospecting."

Many reactive salespeople live by this motto. They will do anything to avoid prospecting, and have learned very well how to do anything but. They know they have to prospect, but how they hate people hanging up or not calling them back, the feeling of being second rate, getting rejected, hearing no, no, and no. It's not a fun task. Salespeople would rather spend time in the Dead Zone or the Maintain Zone, since it is safer than the RedZone; there is less risk and less to fear. But salespeople do need to spend time in the RedZone. Why?

Here are the issues that go along with the RedZone.

- *BA* and *CA* deals are, by definition, going on right now, somewhere. If you are not spending time in the Red-Zone, someone else is getting these deals.
- Prospects need what you have. You are going to help them make money or save money, and the sooner they start, the more money they are going to make.
- Practice the quota trick. Let's say you have a $1,000,000 quota for the year. The trick is not getting to $1,000,000. You have 50 to 75 percent of that number already figured out. The idea is to make up the delta, to close the difference to get to 100 percent of the quota. The point isn't to get the $1,000,000, since most of that quota is coming from somewhere that you have already figured in. The Law of the Sales Person's Prospecting Motto infers that if salespeople do not have to prospect to make their quotas, they won't.
- Look at your planner. At least 30 to 50 percent of your next 90-day activities should be scheduled out as Red-Zone activities. Most of you have planned Dead Zone and Maintain Zone activities hoping these will lead to orders. Keep hoping. Remember the Law of Being Lucky Rather than Good?
- Update your 90-day schedule monthly. Look at your appointments and determine the proportion of Dead, Maintain, and RedZone activities. If it is not what you want it to be, change it.
- It's where the money is. Once you establish yourself and get comfortable in the RedZone, you will be more successful.

You need to find the time to call on your RedZone customers. Now the questions are:

- When should you call on them?
- Who should you call on?
- How much time should you spend in the RedZone?

PowerHour, the next ProActive Selling tool, answers all
these questions and more.

Tool   **PowerHour**^{Tool}

It's Monday morning, first thing. You sit down at your desk,
look at your e-mails, listen to your voice mails, and for the next
few hours, you are reactive. You are marching to someone else's
drum and behaving like a reactive salesperson. This should
make you angry.

Why do you feel the need to be reactive and jump right in
to find out what is waiting for you? Listen to those voice mails?
Read those e-mails? Do you know why you do this? The reactive addiction is kicking in.

Being ProActive is hard. Prospecting is ProActive. Returning someone's call is reactive. Salespeople get into the reactive
addiction more than they should. Take the following Reactive
Salesperson's Quiz:

1. How many voice/e-mails do you get a day?
   a. fewer than 5
   b. between 5 and 15
   c. between 15 and 25
   d. over 25
2. Of the last 10 sales situations you were involved in, how
   many times did the customer basically "take over the
   call" and tell you what to do?
   a. none
   b. 1 to 3
   c. 4 to 6
   d. 7 to 8

     e. all of them, are you kidding, that's what I am there for, to do what the customer tells me to do!

3. Do you have:
   a. one phone and one e-mail address
   b. one phone, one e-mail address, and a cell phone
   c. one phone, one e-mail address, a cell phone, and a pager
   d. office phone, cell phone, pager, e-mail at the office, e-mail at home, fax phone number, laptop, and a palmtop or PDA
   e. multiple of any items of (d)
4. If you ranked your sales situations on an *A, B, C* scale, you would find you spend your time:
   a. 80 percent on *A*s, 10 percent on *B*s, 10 percent on *C*s
   b. 60 percent on *A*s, 30 percent on *B*s, 10 percent on *C*s
   c. 40 percent on *A*s, 30 percent on *B*s, 20 percent on *C*s
   d. 30 percent on *A*s, 20 percent on *B*s, 50 percent on *C*s
   e. 10 percent on *A*s, 20 percent on *B*s, 70 percent on *C*s
5. What percent of the time per week do you spend planning 1 to 3 months out on your day timer, ProActively scheduling time with RedZone appointments?
   a. 20 to 30 percent
   b. 20 percent
   c. 10 percent
   d. 5 percent
   e. I have to make the number TODAY!

If you answered (e) to more than two of the above questions you are addictively reactive and need to do something about it. Welcome to PowerHour.

PowerHour is a discipline. It is how you should spend the first hour of every day. You need to prioritize and march to your own drum the first thing every morning. Spend the first hour of every day marching to your agenda, and not someone else's. Spend it being ProActive, and spend time in the RedZone.

You must spend 1 hour a day, 5 hours a week in the RedZone during PowerHour. This is no big deal. The results, however, will come shining through. Be ProActive and own that first hour. Make it your hour, your RedZone time. Be selfish, make money, face your prospecting fears, it's OK.

PowerHour is not a time for you to:

- Review your schedule for the rest of the day/week/month.
- Organize your thoughts for the day.
- Review some marketing literature.
- Call friends.
- Make a to do list.
- Clean your desk.
- Back up your computer.

PowerHour is designed for you to maximize your time in the RedZone. To do this, you must be very jealous of your time in PowerHour and how you are using it. You need to change your sales prospecting behavior.

To change that behavior and make PowerHour work, you need to go off-site for the first week. Go to your local coffee shop and stay there for an hour, doing something, anything that is RedZone activity. You can:

- Review some annual reports of two or three RedZone customers.
- Make some prospecting calls.
- Call current customers to get names of contacts.
- Send e-mails to people to network contacts at targeted RedZone accounts.
- Follow up RedZone calls with additional activity calls.

There is a host of things you can do ProActively during PowerHour. This is the time you should spend on RedZone activities, especially your *AB* and *AC* prospects. Some examples of other RedZone activities include:

- Breakfast briefings: 30- to 45-minute breakfasts at a hotel with an expert speaker or partner.

- Call a senior manager at a current customer for a reference campaign.
- Do homework on identified RedZone prospects.
- Knock on doors; physically go to three prospects, and knock on their doors between 7:30 and 8:00 A.M., before they start their day. You may be surprised at how you can get some of their time early in the day.
- E-mail blitzes: The probability of getting a response to an e-mail is low, and in general it's best to avoid e-mails. If, however, the e-mail is a targeted one with a specified reference or purpose in mind, it can be a very effective tool.
- Send a book or article on the latest trend to a senior executive. If there is an article about his or her company that highlights what he or she is trying to do, include it with a note on how and why you can make him money.
- Dial for Dollars: Just start dialing anyone within your RedZone account.
- Trade show follow-up: Follow up with your RedZone accounts who went to a trade show. Follow up with the attendee's boss to find out why he or she funded the trip.
- Call some current customers and ask them for leads, or if they know any senior managers in your identified RedZone prospects.

These are just a few ideas on what you could be doing during PowerHour. To get started, be aware that, for most salespeople, their first PowerHour will take about 15 minutes. Then your question is, "What do I do with the rest of my time?" The answer is not to worry. You are trying to break an addiction, a reactive one at that, and you need to stay at that coffee shop for the full hour.

After the first few PowerHours, an hour will not be long enough. Learn how to be ProActive, stay in the RedZone for 5 hours a week, and get that prospecting engine going. Five hours a week is all you need to get rolling on being ProActive. Once you get hooked on PowerHour, you will start to guard this time

Ideas I can implement:

IDEAS	ACTION TO BE TAKEN	RESULTS EXPECTED
1		
2		
3		
4		
5		
6		
7		
8		
9		
10		

Figure 2-1. PowerHour action plan

jealously, and marching to someone else's agenda first thing in the morning will become a second priority.

Make PowerHour time your time—your most effective sales time. Be in the zone, and make this time, 1 hour a day, the difference between being reactively OK and ProActively great. This is behavior modification time, and if you give it 1 month, you'll never go back to being reactive, guaranteed.

PowerHour is a discipline that needs some getting used to, but pays major dividends in getting your prospecting done, your time spent doing something that will pay big dividends in the near term, and your agenda being the one that is marched to, not someone else's. It allows you to take a look at another side of selling . . . the ProActive side.

| Tool | **WarBooks**Tool |

Now that you are armed with PowerHour, your questions become, "OK, so I now have the time and the method to do homework, but what homework is important to gather? How much information is too much and/or not enough? How do I organize this information in a useful state? Who has the time to get so organized?" The answer to these questions is WarBooks.

WarBooks are the physical repository of the information you need on your RedZone accounts. WarBooks are tactical in nature and are broken up into three sections:

1. History
2. Company information
3. Sales strategies

History

What has the history of this account been with your company? What have they purchased before, if anything at all? Who has ordered what from you before, and why? If the prospect has not done work with you before, who have they done business with previously, what have they purchased, and why? This is the section where you build your case on why you should be spending so much of your time with this account.

Company Information

What does this company do? What is important to them? Where can you go to get information on a company? Let's answer Where, What, and Why.

Where
  • Annual Reports
  • Hoovers
  • Prospect's Web site

- Prospect's competitors' Web sites
- Market research information
- Magazines/periodicals
- The prospects themselves

There are a multitude of places to gather company information.

What

You need to gather very specific information about your very important prospects. It's almost like you should know more about the prospects than they know about themselves. To achieve this, you need to answer the seven WarBook questions:

1. What is the customer's annual revenue?
2. What is the customer's annual earnings?
3. What is the 2-year history of revenue and earnings?
4. What is the customer's current market share and market size?
5. What are the projections for market share and market size for the next 2 years?
6. What are the customer's top two competitive advantages, and how do you contribute in making them more competitive?
7. What is the mission of the company, and what are the top three items on the corporate agenda?

Answer the seven WarBook questions, and you will know the what.

Why

Every salesperson knows the trick. It goes like this. Every month, every quarter, a salesperson is working on deals. However, there are one, two, and sometimes even three deals out of the ones that are going to close that are *really* important. These are the ones that are going to make or break the quarter or even the year. These are the ones you do a WarBook on.

As a salesperson, you have the choice to work on RedZone accounts. You can be a solution-oriented, consultative, Pro-

Active salesperson; or you can be a vendor: Put a dollar in; get a Coke. You can vend. Which one are you? Go back to the seven WarBook questions, and try to answer them for your top two prospects. Can you answer all seven questions? If you can, congratulations, you are ProActive. If not, why not?

When you are in front of a senior manager of the company you are calling on, what are you going to do or say? Are you going to break out your brochure? How about getting out that PowerPoint presentation you developed for lower level people? Will you give them a Feature/Benefit overview of your product/service and then ask, "So Ms. Smith, given what we can do, how would we benefit you?" That won't exactly impress them.

You need to know more about your accounts than they do, at all levels of the organization, and the seven WarBook questions can do just that. How long do you think it would take you to gather the WarBook information on your top one or two prospects: a few hours at most? This is time well spent.

Sales Strategy

This is where you use the strategies discussed in this book, as well as any others out there, whether Target Account Selling, Solution Selling, Strategic or Power-Base Selling. Here is where you are strategizing the account to work it ProActively.

Assemble one to three WarBooks at most. No computers are allowed here. WarBooks need to be physical binders on your desk. Go out to Staples or Office Depot and buy three one-inch red binders, and start to assemble your WarBooks. A WarBook is assembled on a per deal basis, not by customer. If you are working on two deals with one customer, you should have two different WarBooks.

A WarBook is also very different than a customer folder. A customer folder, by definition, is a reactive document. You are storing information in a customer folder in case you need it (reactive). A WarBook is a ProActive document; you are using the WarBook in a ProActive manner and need it almost every day. It tells you not only what has been done in the past, but also what you need to do in the future.

You are placing the account strategies you have developed in the WarBook, as well as whatever tools will enable your strategies in the future. The WarBook will become more important to you than your day timer, since WarBooks are the roadmaps to sales success for your RedZone accounts.

An Odd Success from a WarBook

One of our clients, after being trained on ProActive Selling, took the concept of WarBooks quite seriously. Each salesperson was required to have and to work a WarBook diligently. The salespeople quickly understood the value of WarBooks, and it became part of that company's culture as a vehicle to discuss an account internally with all levels of management, as well as the normal salesperson's benefits a WarBook possesses. They achieved a higher degree of success after the sales training, and attributed WarBooks as one of the reasons for the higher than expected sales growth.

One success seemed quite odd. A salesperson relayed a story to us a few months after he had implemented his War-Books. He had closed one of the largest deals in the company's history with a major, targeted account. "It was all due to the WarBook," he claimed.

"What do you mean, we asked? How can a WarBook be the major reason you won a deal?"

"Well," he explained, "I had become so used to carrying my WarBooks around, I started carrying them with me on sales calls. I was in the closing process of this major deal, and I needed to make reference to a discussion we had had with the client earlier. I took out the WarBook I had developed for that client and was in the process of looking up some notes, when the client asked what I was doing, and what was in my book. I explained to him it was my WarBook, and that it was how I was making sure we covered every detail during this sale to make sure he got the most value he could from my company and me. He then started to chuckle and opened up his desk drawer and took out a book, which he called his supplier book. It was used similarly to my WarBook, only from the buyer's perspective. Upon seeing the book, I started to laugh as well. His book on my company and my WarBook on his company were different on the inside, but we had both picked identical covers and were doing a similar type of work. We agreed we must be in sync, since we both had the same taste in book covers, and our rapport with each other at from that point on went to a different level."

"Come on, then a WarBook did not really win you that piece of business."

"No, I guess not" he said. "But I can tell you it made him think I had his best interest in mind over anyone else, and by him knowing how much I cared, it had to play a big part in the sale."

How do you argue with that?

When you get good at WarBooks, they become a powerful tool both inside and outside the organization.

Homework is where great salespeople excel. They know that spending too much time doing homework is avoiding actual prospecting and wasting selling time. If they do too little, they go out unarmed. Homework, like anything else that needs mastery, will be somewhat time consuming up front, but after a while, when a process has been established, will become simple and easy. It should end up being 10 to 20 percent of your overall time, and that includes PowerHour time.

The homework you do for prospecting for new or additional business is a critical part of your success. Homework does not mean spending all your time researching your accounts and never making a call, nor does it mean giving it a cursory once over. A ProActive salesperson spends the right amount of homework on his key RedZone accounts and updating his WarBooks. Once you get a system down, you will not only have more information with you when you prospect, but since information is power, you will be more confident and more insistent on success. Preparation, that is, homework, is the key to success—in sports, music, and in almost everything you do. It is especially true in sales. The ProActive sales person wins . . . period.

Chapter 3

Initiate

Buyers begin their buying process with an *Initial Interest,* which means the salesperson should begin by generating initial interest with a selling phase called Initiate.

For a salesperson to be ProActive, he must master the early part of the sales process, which is much more important than the ending or closing part. For now, forget learning all those closing techniques, and focus on where you can really make a difference. The better a salesperson is in setting up the sale correctly, the better qualified and cleaner the deal is. Therefore, generating initial interest is a very important step in every sale. The overall goal of this phase is to:

- Introduce yourself and your product/service to the customer.
- Interest the customer in your product/service.
- Determine whether there is a reason to continue the process.

That's it. This part of Initiate is very simple, with no pressure or prospecting stress. Too many salespeople believe the goal of Initiate, or prospecting, is to get an order or an appointment. Why would you want to put that much pressure on yourself? The goal of Initiate is simple:

1. Here is who I am and who my company is.
2. Here is what we do and how it could benefit what you do.
3. Should we continue on through a buy/sales process?

If a salesperson has a receptive prospect and thinks the prospect wants to continue on as well, then he should go for it. If the prospect or the salesperson chooses not to continue on, for whatever reason, then the salesperson should try again later with this prospect or move on to another one. It must be a mutual decision.

You are now probably asking yourself,

> *"How can this be a mutual decision? What if they don't return my phone calls or my e-mails? What if they do not get back to me? How can I choose to continue on if they don't get back to me?"*

All these questions will be answered later in this chapter. The current discussion is about the goal of Initiate, and what the overall structure is.

Remember that the goal in Initiate is not to "get an order" or "get a commitment" or "get an appointment." If you shoot for these goals, you will be disappointed. They are too hard, your chance of success is minimal, and, quite frankly, they are very one-dimensional. You are considering only your perspective. Instead, your goal should be to focus on the three goals of this stage: introduce yourself, introduce your product, and determine whether to proceed.

Both the salesperson and the prospect need to determine whether to move forward. It must be a win–win since people have an aversion to being sold at or to. This is easy to say, but very difficult to pull off in practice.

Goals of Initiate

Goal 1: Introduce Yourself

Your first goal is to introduce yourself and your company in a concise, clear, and professional manner. If you have a unique or difficult name to pronounce, be extra careful to enunciate it so the prospect does not have to guess at who you are, and go S . . . L . . . O . . . W. Give the listener time to absorb and think.

Goal 2: Introduce Your Product/Service

This is where you patiently discuss what is currently important to the prospect, and based on previous knowledge gathered through homework or information gathered during this call, try to introduce *in an effective way* what you have to offer the client. This may sound simple, but the approach here is crucial. Too many buyers are literally being attacked by salespeople with their message.

- "Call me back today to discuss what we are all about . . ."
- "I'm sure you would be interested in what we have to offer . . ."
- "Please call me back if what I have said about what we do is of interest to you . . ."
- "You need what we have . . ."
- "Once you understand our value proposition . . ."

These are probably the most common approaches, and none of them are very effective. The goal here is to introduce successfully what you do, so the buyer understands and relates your product to *their* issues and concerns.

Goal 3: Should We Continue on Through a Buy/Sell Process?

Now that you understand the first two goals of generating interest, *both you and the prospect* need to decide whether you should continue at this time. By definition then, this is a mutual buy/sell process. If either the buyer or the salesperson thinks that further action at this time would not be a good idea, then the process should be called off and possibly revisited at a later time. If both decide to continue on, then you should go to the next phase in the process, which is Educate.

Here are some caveats regarding the goals of Initiate:

- Buyers may want to get together but need time to mull it over, so they stall. The reason for most stalls is that you are proposing changing what they do, or what they have scheduled already, and most people are uncomfortable with change. They then propose another time and date for a meeting, say 3 months out, or say it is interesting, and tell you to call back later.
- They might say to go and talk to someone else first and then get back to them.
- They may even try to delay or come up with a "hidden objection" as to why this is not a good time right now.
- They may believe they already have a solution in place that does what you do. A salesperson is rarely going to hear on the phone, "Yes, I am very interested in what you have to say, I'll clear my calendar. What would be a good time for you?" It's time for a reality check.

Buyers may be tentative and may have some interest, but do not want to be sold to. They do not want to change what they are doing, the way they are currently thinking, or the ideas they currently hold dear. So you need to adjust your style and approach to help them through this change, but not adjust the overall goals. You will learn how to help the prospect with these fears later on with some ProActive sales tools.

Once both parties understand that either one can call off this process at any time, the accomplishment of the objectives of Initiate becomes easier. The salesperson may have to push the prospect a little bit to agree to take a next step, but once at that step, called Educate, both the salesperson and the prospect have an easy way out so they don't have to feel pressured.

Finally, the actual work involved in prospecting is never easy, nor is it a tremendous amount of fun. If you are looking for a book or a sales method that will make prospecting a great deal easier, you will not find it here. What this book does show you is how to make your prospecting more effective—far more effective than it has ever been before.

In this phase you need to:

- Determine the prospect's needs.
- Interest the prospect in your offering.
- Summarize, Bridge, and Pull to Educate.

To accomplish these and prospect successfully, you need to do two things:

1. Homework—you need to do the work required before you make any sales contact with a prospect. This was discussed in Chapter 2.
2. The prospecting call itself—the actual contact you make with a prospect

Your homework is done, and you are ready to make some prospecting calls. You know what company to call on, who to call on, what is important to them, and what you are going to say. All you need now before you begin is to make sure your prospecting call is in the right language.

Tool   **Speak the Right Language**Tool

PowerHour is a tool from Chapter 2 to answer the questions of when to prospect and how to use your time most efficiently. The next question you have to ask is, "Whom do I call on?"

You will be using PowerHour to do the homework necessary to make phone calls, as well as to prospect. This can be in person or over the phone, but it is typically a dialog between interested or soon to be mutually interested parties, the seller and the buyer. The physical act of prospecting, dialing the phone or knocking on a door, is something anyone can do. The real issue, or better yet the question that needs to be addressed before you pick up that phone or start to knock on a door, is:

"What do I say to the person when I start talking? I can

dial the phone or go door to door. That's easy. When I get someone on the line or see them face-to-face, what do I say?

How do I begin the conversation so there is an interested in

what I have to say?"

Many salespeople have a fear of prospecting. What they really fear is the frustration and hassle of rejection. Good salespeople know the first minute of prospecting is crucial, since rapport is built early and the conversation follows from that first minute. So why do salespeople avoid prospecting? What is this big fear of prospecting?

FIRST MINUTE OF PROSPECTING FEAR

"You know, my problem is not prospecting. I can do that. My problem is the first minute. If I can get their attention for a minute and then build rapport off of that, then I know I'll be OK. It's that first minute, or even the message I have to leave on voice mail to get someone to call me back . . . that's what I struggle with. Get me past that first minute of conversation, or give me a voice mail message that will get them to call me back, and then I am set."

It is easy to overcome this fear and become very powerful during the first minute of prospecting, as well as during your entire prospecting process. It all hinges on how effectively you communicate to the person you are talking to and on speaking the right language.

There are three levels and, by default, three languages in every organization. Not only do companies speak three languages, but it is also a salesperson's job to speak the right language to the right person at the right time.

The First Level and Language

The first level is the person in the customer's organization you would typically call on all the time. Typical titles these people would have include:

- Manager
- Manufacturing Manager
- Engineer
- Purchasing Agent
- Director
- IT Manager
- Office Manager
- Engineering Manager
- Buyer
- Marketing Manager
- Store Manager

First level buyers are those at the managerial level. Managers speak the language of *Feature/Function*.

- "Does your solution come with training?"
- "Does the system have the latest features on it?"
- "Can I get expedited delivery?"

Figure 3-1. Manager Level

- "How does this compare with last year's model?"
- "Where can I see one working?"

Managers are very interested in the feature/function of the product/solution on its own merits. To sell to managers, salespeople must be able to have a discussion with them and be able to answer their questions. Salespeople therefore are always attending product and services training and reading a ton of company brochures and manuals every chance they get to make sure they do not have to say, "I don't know." Product and technical competence are at issue here, and salespeople want to be fully prepared, so they learn about the product or services they sell. This product/service training translates into:

- Features knowledge
- Feature/benefit statements
- Feature/advantage/benefit statements
- Competitive features
- Product-focused value propositions

Salespeople are given a host of information on these topics, so when they have a dialog with the managers who speak *Feature/ Function*, they can say the right thing to the right people at the right time.

"Our product can do this 20 percent faster than the current product you are using, because our product has a special feature called. . . ."

"Using this new feature on the GL-3000 will allow you to really make the system hum."

"By using our GLM, GSM, and GMAX modules, you will be able to manufacture those parts much faster than before."

"Our methodology and the way we deliver our service to you will allow for a much smoother integration."

The manager level is where most salespeople make their calls and spend most of their time, so it becomes obvious that salespeople need to become very fluent in this language. Company resources therefore are focused on this language since here is where salespeople demand the most from their company. This includes the marketing department as well as other support organizations.

The Second Level and Language

Companies speak a second level language, however. This is the language of most vice presidents. Vice presidents say something like:

"Thanks for coming . . . really, thanks for coming. You are

20 percent faster than xyz . . . I didn't know that . . .

really . . . and you are 30 percent smaller than previous

models . . . really? . . . I didn't know that . . . and you

are x.556.75z compatible . . . really? . . . I didn't know

that . . . wow . . . thanks for coming . . . really . . . thanks

for that information . . . really, thanks . . . BUT . . . If you

can't make me money or save me money, why am I talking

with you?"

For all vice presidents, there are only two reasons to do anything in business, and those are to *increase revenue* or *decrease cost*. How are you going to increase their revenue or decrease their cost?

A vice president is chartered to make corporate goals. Corporate goals are always stated in fiscal terms: earnings, earnings before insurance and taxes (EBIT), net present value of investments (NPV), revenue per employee, compound annual growth rate (CAGR), as well as a host of other fiduciary measurements. A vice president is chartered with the health of the business,

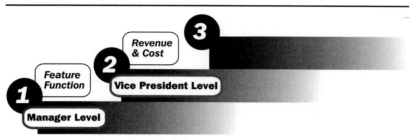

Figure 3-2. Vice President Level

and along with that mandate is the responsibility that all major decisions that affect their organization be fiscally sound ones.

You need to know what a vice president is really interested in as it relates to what you are selling. What is his hot button? What is really important to him? What is he willing to take action on? The answer is *value* and the value proposition. If you remember the value proposition from Chapter 1, what is important to them is *their* value proposition, not yours.

Value proposition from the seller's point of view:

- We have offices in 22 locations around the world.
- It took us 4 years to develop this product.
- We hire only the smartest people.
- We integrate with 85 different systems.
- We have had 22 quarters of positive earnings.
- Our product is 20 percent better than its closest competitor.
- Our corporation is now leading the charge for this industry.

Great, really great, but what is in it for me (also known as WIIFM)? Too many salespeople want to deliver the value proposition of their company and then assume the customer can translate what it means to them. In every conversation you have, whether in business or in your personal life, whenever you let someone interpret the meaning of what you have said, you have a possibility of miscommunication. A ProActive salesperson understands that the vice president wants to know WIIFM. Vice

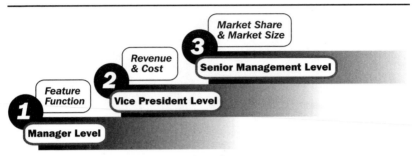

Figure 3-3. Senior Management Level

presidents want to know what is the value for them in your solution.

The Third Level and Language

The third-level language that companies speak is reserved for senior management: presidents, senior vice presidents, executive vice presidents, CFOs, CEOs, CIOs, and so on. At the top of the list of things they care about are market share and market size. That's about it. How big is the market, how big can it get, and how much share of this market can the company get? (How much share can I, the CEO, have, maintain, preserve, take, cover, and develop as well?)

While talking to people at this level, you need to focus on market share and market size. It is their lifeblood, their focus, and their ultimate measure. How much pie is there and how much of that pie can I get? This is what third level managers talk about.

The Three Languages in a Business Process

A real life business process will help illustrate the concept of the three languages. Level 3 managers need to go to their bosses (stakeholders, shareholders, owners, board of directors, and so on) every year and, in most cases, every quarter to report on the state of the business as well as current and future plans. Level 3 managers say to their bosses something like this:

> *"The market is growing 14 percent CAGR over the next 3 years. If you adopt and approve my plans, we will profitably grow the business 3 percent over the next 3 years."*

Unusual circumstances aside, if a president went to his board and made this statement, how long do you think he would be able to keep his job? Not very long, that's for sure. What the president needs to say is:

> *"The market is growing 14 percent CAGR over the next 3 years. If you adopt and approve my plans, we will profitably grow the business 19 percent over the next three years and take significant share away from our competitors."*

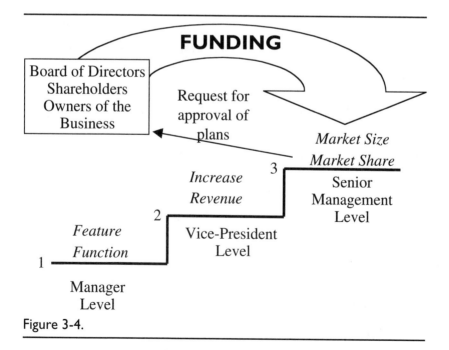

Figure 3-4.

This is a much better picture, and if this happens, and the board/shareholders/stakeholders approve these plans, the president will be funded for another year.

Now that the president has been funded, he goes to his Level 2 managers and gives them *budgets* for the fiscal year and then tells them to manage the budgets so they come in under budget but do not go over. They need to deliver 10 percent more top line (revenue) while holding bottom line (costs) to budget. These are common requests Level 3 managers make to Level 2 managers.

Now that Level 2 managers have budgets, they formulate, reexamine, plot, manipulate, devise, and assign these budgets to different departments in their organization. How are budgets allocated? Which Level 1 manager, who works for the Level 2 manager, has the best *ideas* that are going to help her meet her budgets? The department or the people who have the best ideas to help the vice president make her business goals (budget) will get more than their fair share of the limited resource (money) for the year.

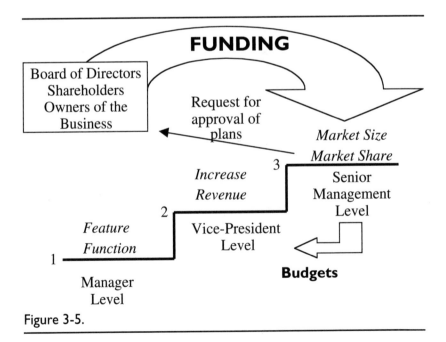

Figure 3-5.

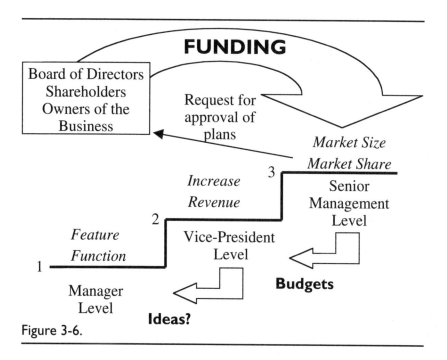

Figure 3-6.

It all plays out from there. The great ideas get more budget money, they help the Level 2 manager make her budget, and since they were great ideas, they did better than budget, and therefore helped the Level 3 manager increase market share. However, what level of language is the most important level to speak? What language is the most productive for the ProActive salesperson to master so he can win more deals and increase his sales? Salespeople must learn to speak the language of the Level 2 manager most fluently, that is the language of Value—value for the customer.

Three Languages: The Reason to Become Multilingual

Before you get into the language of Value, the three languages need to be anchored, since the languages are a concept that most salespeople are aware of, but just do not know what to do with it.

There is a huge push in most sales organizations nowadays to call higher in the organization. Call at the top, at the senior management level. Sell to VITO (very important top officer).

Calling high by itself is not the trick. Anybody can call high. The trick is knowing what to say when you call high in an organization. What do you say to a senior level executive that will let you be seen as a value-add and not just as a salesperson who is trying to peddle something?

An even greater fear a salesperson has is that after meeting with a senior executive, the senior executive thinks the salesperson adds little value to them, and ends up passing the person down in their organization to a lower level. He or she then has to jump through hoops to get back up to the senior level again.

What can you say to add value in these senior management sales calls? First, speak the right language.

Take the three levels of language we just discussed and identify each as a different actual language. For the Level 1 language, the manager level, assign "Spanish," for Level 2, the vice president level, "Russian," and for the senior manager level, Level 3, "Greek." You now have three languages, Spanish, Russian, and Greek.

Imagine you are prospecting at a higher level in a company, at a vice president level, also now called a Russian. You have 1 hour or less to impress and create an interest for what you are selling. You have your usual presentation material, your slides, and projector. You have practiced your speech, your presentation starts, and you are doing great. As a matter of fact, you are quite pleased on how you are really getting into your speech. Having delivered this speech hundreds of times before, you are really good at it.

About 15 minutes into the presentation, however, the vice president interrupts. "Excuse me, but this presentation is in Spanish. I don't speak Spanish very well. Why don't you give this presentation to John and Mary who work for me, since they speak Spanish much more fluently than I do?" This is not what he actually says, but it is what he means.

You are still feeling OK, since the vice president has told you to call John and Mary and you can reference the vice president to get the meeting. You actually can hear yourself making the phone call.

"Hi Mary, this is Chris Ross, and Mr. Hitchcock, your vice president, told me to call you." How much more powerful a reference call can you get? You are thinking you'll get an immediate call back from John and Mary and a sure appointment. You are feeling good about being passed down. What Mr. Hitchcock, the vice president, didn't finish telling you during the call you had with him was what else he was thinking. You were too excited getting his reference to call John and Mary to ask.

"By the way, Chris, I don't speak Spanish anymore, which is the language your presentation is in. I am sure all these feature and functions of what your product does are important to the people who speak Spanish who work for me, so please spend your time with my Spaniards, and they will tell me if what you have is important."

They continue on, "Quite frankly, Chris, I used to speak Spanish, but then I got promoted, and now I speak Russian. I am also very busy trying to learn Greek. Can you help me with that?" This was a golden opportunity to offer the vice president something he is interested in. You've missed your opportunity, however, because you were too busy speaking Spanish to notice.

You are speaking the wrong language to the wrong person. You have no Spanish to Russian dictionary with you on this sales call, and you are out of luck. You prepared the call in Spanish, gave it in Spanish, and delivered it in Spanish. You hang out with Spanish buyers all the time, and you speak very good Spanish. Great, but it doesn't work with Russians. Speak the right language. Speak Spanish to a Spaniard, Russian to a Russian, and Greek to a Greek.

The Five Ways of Creating Value

When you are talking to Russian as well as to Greek buyers, the language of Value is the only language they know. It is imperative that salespeople learn the language of Value because speaking any other language to a Russian or Greek buyer is ineffective and a waste of valuable company resources. There are five ways of creating value, as follows:

- Return on Investment (ROI)
- Time
- Risk

- Motivation
- Brand

That's it. Value can be related in a sales environment through these five value points. It is called the Value Star.

Tool   **The Value Star**^{Tool}

How do these points create value? How can a salesperson use value to sell to the upper levels of an organization? The points on the Value Star will show you the way.

Create the Value: More than ROI

Return on Investment (ROI) is the measure organizations have used for years. It is the common vocabulary companies use to quantify what is important to them. Companies are always trying to increase revenue and decrease cost to maintain and increase their viability. It's their sole purpose for being. Businesses want to grow profitably, and to do this, they must get a return on all the investments they make.

Figure 3-7. The ProActive Value Star

What do you sell? What do you really sell? When we ask salespeople this question, we usually get answers like:

- Solutions
- Services
- Features and benefits
- Advantages
- A better way of doing something
- Value
- A total package
- Competitive advantages

To sell value, you must know there is only one thing you really sell: You sell money!

When involved in a purchasing decision, senior level people care only about the return they are getting on their investment. That is it. It is all about money. Most Russians and Greeks are greedy. They want even more than just the amount of money they are "giving" you. They want more than their original investment back. They want two to three times the money they are giving you so they can invest that money into other ideas, so they can make even more money. It sounds simple, and it is, and it is based on the premise that you sell money.

One of our clients sells an annual service. It is a subscription-based service for which they charge their customers anywhere from $10,000 to $1,000,000+ per year. The vice president of sales told us once that he had a revelation one day. Here he was trying to sell his company's services and renew subscriptions every year. He thought he was actually selling a service. "If the client paid us $200,000 per year, and we gave them $200,000 worth of our services, I thought everyone was happy." With this thought, the vice president thought he was giving a fair service for a fair price.

"But then I realized that to senior people in the client organization I was just an investment they were making. Seems that they looked at our services differently than the users of our services look at us. Users of our services liked and appreciated what we did, our customer service, our methodology, the way we delivered information, and the way we improved on ways of doing things. Senior managers, however, have a different viewpoint. They view us as an investment, and they are interested in only one thing: How they are going to get their money back? What is the return on the investment (ROI) they are making? Oh, I'm sure they like us and think that our stuff is neat and cool, but all they care about is their investment."

"As a matter of fact, now that I know that I sell money, I can see that most of my customers are greedy. They want more than their money back. They actually want a return on their investment. They demand two to three times the money they pay us, because their goal is to make as much money as they can, so then they can invest that money and make more money."

Later on, talking with that same vice president a few weeks later, it was a very different conversation. "I went back and changed my entire PowerPoint presentation. I looked at what I had, and I was not speaking money. I was speaking Spanish. I now realized I must carry a Russian and Greek message when I call on senior managers. Now, when a salesperson goes on a sales call and needs someone to speak at a high level, they bring me. I am seen as a value-add on senior sales calls, and its only because I speak money and ROI. I speak Russian."

ROI is the language the senior management team uses to talk about all investments the company is making, including the purchase of your goods/services. But ROI is a language salespeople do not feel comfortable discussing, since they really believe it is none of their business.

> *"I just tell them what they are buying. Soft dollars or hard dollars? I have no idea. It's up to them to figure out if they can justify it or not."*
>
> *"Can the prospect afford our solution? We are waiting to hear from them on this very issue right now. Personally, I have no idea what they are using to quantify the decision in financial terms, but I sure hope they can afford us."*

"ROI? It's not on one of my slides. I know our product and how the customer is supposed to use it. My bottom line is that I'll cut them a deal they will just find too hard to pass up."

The salesperson who refuses to learn and discuss ROI will be the one who tries to sell on *Feature/Function*. This works for a Spaniard, but Russians have a different agenda.

A final note on ROI: Senior managers can make numbers look almost any way they want them to look. ROI is the method used most often to define value, but it is probably one of the least firm value points on the Value Star. You have to know ROI, talk ROI, and work with ROI, but be ready to play with all the numbers. You have to challenge assumptions and get to the real meat of the ROI analysis. Senior managers need to look at:

- Return on Assets
- Return on Capital
- Net Present Value
- EBIT
- Return on Equity

These are very important measures to a senior manger, and if you want to speak the right language, it may be time to brush up on some of those financial principles.

Time: The Value Leverage

Time is the second point in the Value Star, and with it comes a great deal of leverage. Time has many dimensions to it, and salespeople need to look past their single point of reference for time.

Time can be measured or quantified in many ways:

- Uptime
- Overtime
- Time to market

- Timing of the market
- Just in time
- Right timing
- Time in market
- Downtime
- In time
- Phasing out over time
- Timing the launch of a product

Anyone will pay for time, including you. You will pay more to drive on a toll road and get somewhere quicker than taking the back streets to your destination. That would take too much time. People will pay more to take a direct flight than a stopover if they have a choice. Customers will pay to be faster, quicker, and more rapid than they have been before.

Find out what is important to your customer from a time perspective. You will find there are multiple time elements in most decisions. One person has certain time issues, and another person within the buying organization has other time issues that are very different from those of the first person. Companies have many time constraints, deadlines, and time to market issues. Your job as a ProActive salesperson is to find out as much as you can about the time issue your prospect has.

You cannot cheat time. Customers have only 24 hours in a day, 7 days in a week, 52 weeks in a year. There is no getting around it. Since it is a scarce and valuable resource, prospects value it highly. Find out what is important to them. It could be:

1. Getting a new product to market before a deadline
2. Getting a new product to market before a competitive offering
3. Getting a new product to market before a compelling event (trade show, financial briefing, and so on)
4. Getting new pricing out
5. Getting new packaging out
6. A new reorganization coming up
7. A reorganization that just happened
8. Goals managers have set with their bosses that have time elements to them

9. Doing something in less time

10. Timing issues due to customer relationships

The time list can go on and on. You want to have multiple bullets for the proverbial value gun, so make sure you have multiple time value issues. The more you have, the harder it is for the buyer to say no. Make it worth their time.

Risk: What It Is ALL About

Here lies the key to the kingdom. Value can mean different things to different people, and the objective and subjective nature of ROI and time can debated. Will they save that much time? How do they know they will actually get that kind of ROI? What if the schedule slips? Subjectivity and qualitative factors start creeping in, and the question becomes how do you know where to put the stake in the ground? If you are looking for *the* key value point on the Value Star that rises above them all, the bread and butter play, then look no further. You must talk, understand, and assist prospects in addressing and minimizing their risks.

Risk is the key value factor that keeps senior executives up at night. Decisions at the lower level of the organization are quite binary—black and white, yes/no, now/later, up/down, or in/out. Decisions at the higher levels of companies are never that simple, which is why they need the involvement of a senior executive in the first place. Senior management decisions are much more complex and take into account so many other factors that they are fraught with risk. Risk is what makes senior executives turn their heads and take notice.

"Was there something we forgot? Is there a market out there that someone forgot about, and therefore our current decisions are riskier?"

"Was everyone who needed to be involved, involved? Is there a potential for a communication breakdown that will grind this organization to a screeching halt?"

"Are we making the wisest choices with the limited resources

we have?"

Senior managers want and need to talk about risk. Sales-people come in and talk to them, or at them, all the time. They ask questions, but not the right ones. They ask:

"What would your role be if your company wants to

implement our solution?"

"Are you the final authority for deciding on this

implementation?"

"I wanted our senior manager to meet with you. Is

this OK?"

"We have been working with some of your people, and

we just want to make sure we get your input."

"How do you see our relationship going forward?"

Are these the types of questions that are keeping Russians and Greeks awake at night? Risk is what matters to them. They need to make many decisions daily, and none of them have a 100 percent confidence factor, which is why these decisions and their risks keep senior managers awake at night. It is all about risk.

"What do you see as the biggest risk in a decision like this

to you and your company?"

"What have you thought about regarding this implementa-

tion and where you can minimize your risk?"

"How can we, working together, increase the probability of

a successful outcome?"

"What do you see as the major risk factor with this project?"

"What are the risks you face in the next 3 to 6 months re-

garding this solution?"

Senior executives are eager to talk to you about risk. It is what they face daily, yet no salesperson wants to discuss it with them. Salespeople come into the office and try to sell something, usually speaking Spanish, and spew out a *Feature/Function* presentation. Russians and Greeks care about value, and they really care about the risks their decisions are going to have on the organization.

"What are the risks associated with launching this new

product now instead of next quarter?"

"If I shut down capacity at this factory for a month to

add this new piece of equipment, what are the start up

risks associated with that?"

"What will the risks be to all of my departments if I add

this new process into the organization?"

Senior managers make decisions all they time. That's why they are senior managers. For every decision they make, every investment they have to make, for every act they have to justify, they have to weigh the risks. Make a Russian or Greek's decision safer, or less risky, and you will have their attention.

Motivation: The Delivery

Value must be communicated in either a TOWARDS or AWAY language. The motivation of the prospect has a direction, and that direction is unique to each buyer in the prospect's organization. Motivational direction and how buyers buy was discussed in Chapter 1. Value must also follow these motivational direction rules. Expressing value to a TOWARDS prospect in an AWAY mode will not work.

The best example of this is when salespeople are telling a potential customer how much cost they will cut out, how much they will eliminate, or how much they will save them if they buy their product/service. Because this is spoken in an AWAY direction, it works for 70 percent of the buyers. Remember, though, there are 30 percent of buyers who could care less about saving costs or time. Their mission is to increase revenue and make time available for something else.

When communicating value, remember to put it in the right motivational direction. If you have to guess, speak to both directions or go with the odds and speak AWAY (70 percent).

Brand/Image: The Wrapping Paper and Bow

The final point on value star is Brand/Image. Brand/Image also includes quality, since quality is usually in the eye of the beholder, and is more perception than reality.

Brand/Image takes shape in the form of:

- The product
- The company
- The customers you have
- The salesperson and sales manager
- The company history
- The marketing literature
- The customer support you offer
- The Web site you maintain
- The last sale you made
- The contract you ask the customer to sign
- The proposal you gave the customer
- The letters and e-mail you use to correspond with the customer
- The logo of your company

The list can be endless. Value is very individualistic. Brand/Image is where emotions and perceptions come into play, and you need to find out what is really important to each buyer in the prospect's organization.

Brand/Image plays to perceptions. It can be as simple as, "I always buy a Sony, since I know the quality will be high" to "I trust Lisa and her company. Her professionalism has been demonstrated throughout this evaluation."

In the first example, the Brand/Image is based on reputation and past history, but it still is a personal, emotional rationalization. In the second example, the Brand/Image is based on the actions of the salesperson and how she represents her company. Remember that in both examples, the prospect is transferring this idea of Brand/Image to their own decision-making process. It's as if the prospect is saying to themselves,

"Since I am buying from Lisa or from Sony, I am like them.

I have a perception that I want to be associated with, and

Sony or Lisa represent my idea of Brand/Image I want other

people to judge me by."

Emotional ownership transfers with Brand/Image, and it can be personal or organizational.

Also discuss with your customers what your product/service will do for *their* Brand/Image. If you can improve *their* competitiveness, make them look better by associating with you, or lessen the risk of *their* customers who buy *their* products, you create leverage, and create value. Think from your customers' perspective as well as yours.

The Value Star is a unique way of defining how salespeople should arm themselves ProActively and sell what the buyer is asking for, not what the seller wants to sell them.

Value Star Defined

A friend, Xavier Zang, puts it this way. The Value Star is like a present. The present itself is ROI, Time, and Risk. These are the big three from which you can get quantifiable results. If anyone tells you they are having a tough time quantifying a deal, go to these three. There are no "soft dollars" problem with these three. The next one, Brand/Image, is like the wrapping on the gift. Brand/Image is how you are going to package the value to the buyer or the buying organization. Motivation is the delivery mechanism. How are you going to deliver this package, in a TOWARDS or AWAY (or both) form in your presentations and proposals? This is a rather unique concept, but he remembers to use all five points of the Value Star in his dealings.

The Value Star is your key to being multilingual in a prospect's organization. If you spend half the time learning the key areas of the Value Star that you spend learning product knowledge and *Feature/Function* knowledge, imagine how fluently you could sell to value. Figure 3.8 is a worksheet you can use to start expanding your Value vocabulary.

Finally, you may find yourself in a meeting at which multiple languages are being spoken at the same time. You may have a few Spaniards and a Russian in a meeting, and sometimes even a Greek shows up. The question most salespeople have at this juncture is, "What language do I speak in the meeting?"

The answer is always to speak up; speak to the higher level. When a Spaniard is in a meeting with a Russian, you need to speak Russian. Managers know they must speak the language of their bosses to get promoted. Good managers know that if they want to get their project approved or to even be considered for a promotion, they need to become multilingual and learn Russian. How many times have you been in a meeting with a Spaniard and a Russian, and the Spaniard only wants to speak in Spanish, and the Russian gets annoyed since she is left on her own to translate between Spanish and Russian? Worse, there are times where there are multiple Spaniards in the room, and they want to dominate the conversation and not even let you get a word in with the Russian. (I call this a Spanish Inquisition. The Spaniards dominate the conversation by asking a host of *Feature/Function* questions, and you are forced to speak in Spanish during the entire presentation.)

It is the wise Spaniard who can translate Spanish into Russian for the vice president, since the vice president will view that Spaniard as someone who is credible and thinks the right way. The Russian then looks differently at this particular manager, since the Russian believes this Spaniard has the ability to think

What are the business
risks the person you are
calling on faces in the
next 6–12 months?

Risk

ROI   **Time**

What is the solution
quantifiably worth to the
buyer?

What are the critical time
issues the person you are
calling on faces currently?

Brand   **Motivation**

What does the buyer associate
you with? What do you want
them to associate you with?

What is the person's pain
or vision they are trying to
address?

1. ROI Answer-

2. Time Answer-

3. Risk Answer-

4. Motivation Answer-

5. Brand Answer-

Figure 3-8. The ProActive Value Star worksheet.

like a Russian and see things from a Russian's perspective. That Spanish person who can say what he wants or what the need truly is in Russian gets what he wants and is also considered promotable.

When in doubt, speak up. Speak the right language to the right person, and you will communicate your product/service value proposition much more powerfully than ever before.

Armed with the knowledge of who should you call on and what should you say, you are now ready for your first sales call. It is time actually to prospect.

The Initial Sales Call: Overcoming the Fear

Prospecting is an emotionally charged word. Salespeople will do so many things, go through so many hoops, and go to absolutely amazing lengths when they are involved in a sale, and then relish in the stories afterwards of what they had to go through to get a sale. Selling is fun. Getting a sale is fun. You love selling.

Change the subject to prospecting, and you get an entirely different narrative. Prospecting is frustrating. Selling is fun, but most salespeople would rather just sell and take the word prospecting out of their vocabulary. Some salespeople claim to love to prospect; most dislike it, and dislike is a mild word for how they really feel.

> *"Prospecting is something I have to do to get the sale*
>
> *going. I hate it, and I am not good at it."*
>
> *"Prospecting is tough. It's tough to take all those 'no*
>
> *thank you' calls and even tougher to take someone*
>
> *not even bothering to call you back. It makes you feel*
>
> *so insignificant, so second class."*

"If I can just get past the first minute or so of a prospecting call, then I'm fine. It's that first minute of building rapport and creating an interest that I just can't get past."

With attitudes like these, it is easy to see why salespeople would rather avoid the whole prospecting arena. Prospecting is never easy, but you first need to put the entire issue of prospecting into place. The law of prospecting is simple, yet controversial.

THE LAW OF PROSPECTING

If you want to have customers in the pipeline, you have to prospect. If you want good prospects in your pipeline, you have to do it yourself.

Salespeople and organizations will expend a huge amount of energy and resources to get prospects. They divide their attention among lead generation, lead generation activities, qualified leads, initial sales discussions, initial contacts, trade show leads, and reference leads. The list could keep going. Here are some basic facts regarding prospecting.

- If you want good prospects, you are going to have to hunt for them yourself, period.
- Most salespeople would rather do ANYTHING other than prospect . . . and they will come up with every justifiable reason in the book why today is not the right day to prospect—the stars are not aligned right, the marketing material is inadequate, or they are just not yet ready to do a good job at it.
- Other activities to gather key names and opportunities are good homework and can be done by others. Inbound sales qualification can be done by an inside sales team. The actual contact to the customer, however, especially at the senior level, should come from the salesperson.

- Marketing activities to get leads are worthwhile. The key is they have to be expressed in the right language and have a call to action. More marketing dollars should be allocated to getting leads into the sales team than to support sales funnel activity.
- Trade shows can be a good source of leads. Most companies do a poor job at working a trade show and talking to attendees at the show with the sole purpose of generating leads at and beyond the show's reach. How many salespeople get a lead from a trade show and call the person who was attending to ask their interest? It's less than 20 percent. How many salespeople call that attendee's boss, who allocated money for the attendee to go to the show and speak Russian, rather than Spanish, to the boss? It's fewer than 5 percent. It's all in the effort.
- Prospecting must be a comfortable unconsciously competent process. If a salesperson wants to be good at it, she has to do it a lot.
- Prospecting must be a part of a sales team's culture. Rewards must be set for good prospecting activities, not just for final revenue results.
- Prospecting is mostly a mental attitude, a belief. There are tactics that can be used to be good at it, but salespeople who are good at prospecting *believe* they are good at it. In reality, they may be mediocre, but if they really believe they are good and constantly work at being good, that enthusiasm comes across to the prospect. Prospecting is easy if you have the right attitude and goals in mind.
- Nonverbal communication comes across the phone in volumes. Sit up when you are prospecting at your desk, and smile. Use a mirror; it is hard not to smile when you are looking at yourself in a mirror.
- Prospecting should be fun. You are trying to contact people who are going to make you money, and you are going to make them money. It's in the attitude. Have a good time.

The Mental Attitude of Prospecting

Most pro sports players say that to master the sport they play and become the best in the world at it, is all about mental attitude. In tennis, for example, most of the top 20 tennis pros, men and women, have the shots. They have the physical talent to take them to the top 20 in the world. They say that what is required of them to be number one and stay number one is mental toughness and mental focus. They believe they are great and will win. There is no way they will lose.

Successful prospecting is a mix of homework, talent, and attitude. You have already learned about the homework required of a ProActive salesperson, and you will be getting tools a salesperson can use to be better on initial sales calls. Right now, however, it is the attitude that counts. A salesperson must have the correct, positive attitude toward prospecting. What is this right attitude? What is in it for them?

The reason salespeople prospect is to make a sale. This is a very straightforward and one sided, but a nonproductive way to look at prospecting. Prospecting with the goal of having to make a sale puts a tremendous amount of pressure on a salesperson.

> *"If I don't get this person to call me back, then I won't make a sale, and I won't make my number for the month, then I won't make my quota, then I will get fired, then I will be out of work and have to look for a new job . . ."*

Salespeople who are good at it have the right Prospecting Attitude:

> *"I am contacting you because I believe you have a need. I may be able to make you money and solve a big problem for you. We might be able to help you satisfy that need. Let's have a*

conversation to see if there is a mutually beneficial reason

for us to get start a discussion."

A quick reminder is that a need and the satisfaction of this need are directly dependent on what level you are calling on. A Spaniard, Russian, and Greek have very different needs. They should all be approached in the same manner, but what you say to each should directly relate to the three languages.

Timing is a critical element as well. Even in the right language, when you are the recipient of a prospecting call, and you don't need what is being discussed with you at that moment when a salesperson is prospecting and calling on you, what you are really saying is your motivation is not high right now, and you say no "thank you" to the caller. The salesperson says you are not a prospect and never calls you again. There's no reason for this, but what has happened is that the salesperson believed that he or she had been rejected by the prospect, and the salesperson will not call them back ever again.

Too many salespeople say something like, "I called him a year ago, and there was no interest. I am not going to waste my efforts on that guy again." This is a poor prospecting attitude. The timing was not right, but the salesperson takes it personally and does not have the right prospecting attitude.

The right prospecting attitude must be,

"Hi, this is what we do, and based on some homework I

have done, this is what you do. Is there a reason for us to

get together?"

If the answer is no, and your initial homework is sound, it can be:

- Wrong timing: Try again in a month.
- Wrong person: You need to find the person with the motivation.
- Wrong approach: What language are you speaking?

The tactics of placing or executing a well-executed first call are coming up. For now, salespeople must believe. Their attitude must be that they are prospecting to assist both sides mutually. Remember the number one prospecting premise:

> *There will always be a sale, since everything someone wants, someone else has.*

Armed with this, you owe it to your prospects to make what you are selling available to them.

The Prospect's Perspective

If you are prospecting and have the right attitude, then why is it so hard for prospective customers to agree to spend time with you if you really have the ability to help them out? Remember you are asking someone, the prospect, to do something he or she hates to do. Most salespeople and prospects alike HATE to change.

You are asking someone to change what they are currently doing, currently evaluating, and currently in process with, and potentially to take a risk. Change takes a lot of work, time, and hassle. People like patterns, repeatability, generalizations, rationalizations, and so on. Who wants more work, which is the work required to change?

Prospects fear change—it carries risk. Your goal is to understand prospects before you make your first contact. Assume that they are skeptical of change, and work with them instead of calling on them and inundating them with *Feature/Benefit* statements. Understand that their desire to change is low in the beginning of a buy/sell process, and start your sales effort from the prospect's perspective, not yours.

The second part of Initiate, the actual sales call, is the next step in the process. You are armed with your homework and are in the right prospecting state of mind, so it's time for your first call.

Chapter 4

How to Begin and End Every Sales Call

Your homework is done, and you are well prepared. You are in the right prospecting frame of mind. You can't stall anymore. It is time to get out there and start selling. It is prospecting time.

The goals of Initiate were discussed earlier. They are:

- Introduce yourself (Goal 1): The Beginning
- Introduce your product/service (Goal 2): The Middle
- Determine whether to continue on through a buy/sell process (Goal 3): The End

This stage of the sales process is very straightforward and has no "have to get the sale" pressure. If you follow these three goals, your prospecting ability will improve. This is easier said than done, of course, but here are some tools for you to use to get better at implementing the overall goals of the initial call, or in simple terms, prospecting.

Look at the three goals. They all seem very simple in their own right, and they are. The sales novice can execute these goals as easily as the experienced salesperson. The goal that usually gets the most attention is Goal 2—introducing your product/service. The salesperson gets the most training on this, the most marketing support, and uses this information the most. The thinking is that, if you know the product or service you sell so well, you can be self-reliant and have to depend only on yourself to earn a living.

But you are spending time learning the least important of the three goals. In-depth product knowledge helps only when you are calling on a manager. At the vice president or CEO level, it is all about sales call control, and control of the call is at the beginning and the end: starting off the call in control and directing the prospect to do what you want him or her to do, and at the end of the call, again wanting the prospect to do what you want him or her to do. The middle, what you have so much knowledge on, is the filler that you seem never to get quite enough of. Control of the sales call is mastered by flawless execution of Goals 1 and 3.

Goal 1, *Introducing yourself*, seems on the surface to be very easy, as does Goal 3, *Should we continue on through a buy/sell process?* The intent of these goals is to tell the customer who you are, and at the end, determine whether you have a prospect that is worth your time. Executing these goals is easy, and a salesperson would rather focus on product knowledge than on the other goals since Goals 1 and 3 seem so simple, so easy. It is at Goals 1 and 3 where you will either win or lose a sale, since it is not about your product at the upper two levels; it is about control.

Goal 1: Introduce Yourself— The Beginning

At this stage you introduce yourself and try to get the prospect interested enough in what you are saying to start having a conversation with you. For you to be any good at this, you must make a good first impression. Either on the phone or in person, an initial contact has to be made, and a first impression is going to be established.

How long do you think you have to make a first impression? Most people would say a minute or two. The answer is 4 to 6 seconds. In 4 to 6 seconds, your brain is taking information in and starting to filter (generalize, distort, delete) the information that is coming into it. A second question is: How long do you think you have to gain or lose credibility? You have roughly 30 to 40 seconds. After that amount of time, your brain, as the listener, now starts asking questions and wants to participate, either positively or negatively. How would you like to be able to, in 30 to 40 seconds:

- Make a good first impression?
- Introduce yourself?
- State your business case so the buyer remembers it?
- Get your buyer to agree to your business case?
- Get the buyer's interest and attention?
- Have them start talking and begin having a meaningful business discussion with you?

Welcome to the 30-second speech.

Tool   **The 30-Second Speech**Tool

The first tool you will learn to prospect successfully with is the 30-second speech. Many salespeople call this an elevator speech, but it is much more than that. A good 30-second speech is the only way a salesperson should start out every prospecting sales call. It allows the salesperson to start out every prospecting effort in control. A 30-second speech should go like this:

> *Good morning Mr. Grega. My name is Mary Jones. I am the salesperson for the ABC Company. At ABC, we are a leading provider of software and services for sales force automation systems. We provide tools that help salespeople shorten their sales cycles and qualify better. We also help sales managers get to 90 percent forecast accuracy in about half the time. Questions we get all the time from sales vice presidents like yourself are, "Is there a way to really make salespeople more productive?" "Can I really get the maybes out of my funnel that are causing me to spend resource where I shouldn't?" and "Is there really a way to get my forecasts to 90+ percent accuracy?" We hear these ques-*

> *tions quite a bit, Mr. Grega, but before we get into them, what are the issues and questions regarding your sales team's productivity that are on your agenda currently?*

This is a 30-second speech, and it is a good one. Let's break it down to some basic elements so we can see how to put one together.

A 30-second speech consists of three elements and a conclusion.

Element 1: The Introduction

Simply put, this is where you introduce yourself and your company. This is the time to keep it simple and brief. "Hi, this is who I am, and this is our company," then stop. Right now there

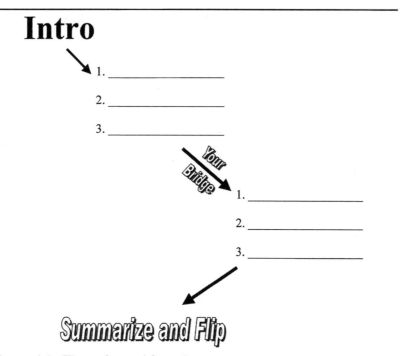

Figure 4-1. Thirty-Second Speech.

is no need to go any further than that. Here is an example of what you would not do:

> *"Hi Mr. Jones, my name is Laura Smith and I am the East-*
>
> *ern Region Account Sales Territory Manager for the ABC*
>
> *Division of the XYZ Company, headquartered in Hamilton,*
>
> *New Jersey, and with offices around the world."*

The question that needs to be asked for an introduction like the one above is: Besides the salesperson, who cares? Why would you want to waste someone's time by telling them all about you? They don't care about you; they care about themselves. Get through this Introduction part quickly and easily. You will have time during the sales call, if need be, to tell them more about you and your company, if they are interested. Keep the Introduction short and sweet, so you can get to the messages you need to get into during your 30-second speech.

> *"Hi, Mr. Jones, my name is Laura Smith, and I am with*
>
> *the ABC Company."*

Element 2: About Us

Now is the time to tell the prospect about you. Keep it short as well, and limited to three things. Why three? Your brain's short-term memory holds seven digits, plus or minus two. This is why we always want things in threes or fives.
  Threes:

- Small/medium/large
- Good/better/best
- First, second, third
- Before/during/after
- Yesterday/today/tomorrow

Fives:

- X-Small/small/medium/large/X-large

- A/B/C/D/F (grades in school)
- Excellent/good/average/poor/very poor

Threes and fives are what people remember, so for Element 2, you want three things about what you do to make an impression. It would be taxing from a timing issue to try to get through five, so stay with three. These three things in Element 2 are called anchors. What's an anchor?

An anchor is something you associate with. For example, answer the following questions:

- What is the safest car in the world?
- Who is number one in the car rental business?
- Where can you go to eat where they have big yellow arches?

If you answered Volvo, Hertz, and McDonald's, you have these as anchors. How do you know that Volvo is the safest car? If you answer, "Volvo says that they are," you are right. Did you know that Volvo has never ranked as the safest car according to many automotive magazines?

How do you know that Hertz is number one in the car rental business? Right again, they tell you they are. How do they measure that? Is it by number of cars rented? Number of active rental outlets? Total revenue of the corporation? You don't really know, but what you do know is that they are number one. Who is number two in the car rental business? You probably answered Avis. How do you know they are number two? Typically people say, "Because they try harder." How do they try harder? Do they run after you when you check your car in? Smile larger? What do they do? You don't know, you just know they try harder.

Other great anchors you may know are:

- Think Different—Apple Computer
- Have It Your Way—Burger King
- Fly the Friendly Skies—United Airlines
- The Real Thing—Coca-Cola
- The Ultimate Driving Machine—BMW

The list goes on and on. Anchors are very powerful, and you may want to develop some for your company. You want to have a list of 10 to 20 anchors available for a 30-second speech, so you can use the one that's right for the specific call you are making. Usually, your anchors won't change too often, but when you are speaking to a CEO, for instance, have Greek anchors ready. It will keep their interest and let them know right up front they should continue paying attention to you.

Element 3: About Them

After you create three brief anchors about you, you want to shift the discussion to the prospect because, quite frankly, it's all about them. You want to now interest the prospect in terms they can understand and get them interested enough to start a discussion. After the first minute or so, the salesperson's goal is to have the prospect interested and to build enough rapport during the prospecting call so a basic business discussion can begin.

It is now time to get the prospect's interest and capture enough of their interest so they start to have a conversation with you, from which you can determine the appropriateness of a next step with this client. For you to accomplish both these objectives, getting their interest and getting them involved with the conversation, you need Element 3, in a questioning format.

Questions get the prospect to think. If they are good questions, which mean ones relevant to the prospect, they will think:

"Yes, these are questions I ask myself all the time. I wonder

if this person really understands my issues."

"Yes, these are some of my issues, and there are some other

ones I really would like to have the answers to as well.

This person is in the right ballpark; maybe they have

some answers."

"No, these are not the questions I ask myself, but they

are close. Let's talk about it."

Any way you look at it, the prospect has to think and get involved when you are asking questions. Two questions you now are asking are:

1. "What are good and relative questions?"
2. "What kind of questions do I ask?"

The answer to the first question is easy. You have already done some homework on this prospect based upon the topics you uncovered in the previous chapters. Use this homework effort to formulate great questions. It does not take that long and can be well worth the investment of a few minutes of time to find out what the prospect is up to before you make that first call. The other area to formulate your questions from is the Three Levels of Language tool. You already know what is important to what level of buyer. Assume for an instance you are calling a vice president (Why would you be calling any lower on a first call?). What is important to a vice president? It's Value of course; increase revenue and decrease cost. So assemble your questions around the Value Star. Ask questions about ROI, Time, and Risk. Find out what they are doing to become more competitive so they make more money, and ask questions in these areas. What you will find out after a while is that all vice presidents, or Russians, have similar issues; it's why they speak the same language—Value. Once you get good at this, the questions will start to flow with very little homework.

The second question, "What kind of questions do I ask?" is easier than the previous question. Remember, *it's all about them.* They are interested in themselves, and not in you yet. So why would you ask questions that pertain to you? *They don't care* about you. So ask the classic WIIFM (What's In It For Me) questions.

WIIFM QUESTIONS—QUESTIONS THAT ARE ON THE PROSPECT'S MIND

"How can I increase revenue in the short term with little or no further investment?"

> *"How can I get my product to market faster than I am currently on track to do?"*
>
> *"Is there a way to lower my risk on the key two or three decisions I am making over the next 6 months?"*

Element 3 asks questions. Questions get the prospect involved and motivated to talk with you. It's why they will allow you to talk with them, because they have questions. It goes to the Law of Questions.

THE LAW OF QUESTIONS

No executive or prospect will ever agree to meet with you because you have something to tell them. They don't care. They will only agree to meet with you because they have a question they need an answer to. Get the question out, not the information in.

Ask great questions to get their questions and issues out on the table, and then start a dialog; and they should be WIIFM questions.

The transition between Element 2 and Element 3 is called a bridge. You have to create a bridge between Element 2 and 3 to transition to the questions. Bridge phrases can be:

"Executives like yourself are always asking us . . ."

"Companies we talk to are asking . . ."

"Major clients like yourself are always asking . . ."

"People in your position are always asking us . . ."

"Some homework I have done on your company shows you are probably asking yourself . . ."

"You are probably wondering . . ."

"You probably are asking yourself on a daily basis . . ."

Use whatever bridge phrase you feel comfortable with. It does not really matter which one you use; it matters that you have a bridge phrase. Putting together the three elements of a 30-second speech now sounds like this:

ELEMENT 1: INTRODUCTION

Good morning, Mr. Grega. My name is Mary Jones. I am the salesperson for the ABC Company.

ELEMENT 2: ABOUT US

At ABC, we are

1. *A leading provider of software and services for sales force automation solutions.*
2. *We provide tools that help salespeople shorten their sales cycles and qualify prospects better.*
3. *We also help sales managers get more than 90 percent forecast accuracy in about half the time.*

BRIDGE PHRASE

Many of the questions we get from sales vice presidents like yourself are,

ELEMENT 3

1. *"Is there a way to really make salespeople more productive?"*
2. *"Can I really get the maybes out of my funnel that are causing me to spend resource where I shouldn't?"*
3. *"Is there really a way to get my forecasts to 90+ percent accuracy?"*

SUMMARIZE AND FLIP

We hear these questions a lot, Mr. Grega, but before we get into these questions, what are the issues and questions regarding your sales team's productivity that are on your agenda currently?

| Tool | **Flip**^{Tool} |

Summarize and Flip is the way you end the speech. You summarize the questions you have asked, and then Flip^{Tool}. A Flip is a tool to get the prospect to start talking. A Flip is asking a question that needs to be addressed by the other person. You need to Flip the 30-second speech at the end so the prospect starts talking. Flipping is one of the top five characteristics of a top salesperson, as outlined in *ProActive Sales Management.* Flipping is remembering to ask questions so the prospect can get involved and start to talk. Flipping makes sure the prospect feels included, and the salesperson does most of the listening.

There you have the schematics of a good 30-second speech introduction. Some basic rules:

- Do not just jump in with a 30-second speech. There usually are a few moments of idle conversation. Pace yourself. Example of introductions are, "Is this a good time for you?" (the permission call) or, "Mr. Patel asked me to call you" (the reference call), or "I was doing some homework on your company and discovered there may be a reason . . ." (the homework call). Whatever your style is, use what you feel comfortable with.
- When you are leaving a voice mail, make sure you spend time on Element 3. When most salespeople leave a voice mail, they do a good job at the Introduction and the three anchors. Then they ask for a callback and forget the WIIFM questions, which is why they are getting a low call back ratio.

> ## THE USUAL VOICE MAIL CALL
>
> *"Hi Ms. Petersen, my name is Gary Willis and I am a salesperson for the ABC Company. The ABC company is*
>
> **1.**
> **2.**
> **3.**
>
> *This is what we do. If this is of interest to you, please call me back at . . ."*

Who would call back with this seller-centric voice mail? A much more powerful 30-second voice mail would be to include Element 3, the WIIFM questions.

> ## THE NEW 30-SECOND SPEECH VOICE MAIL CALL
>
> *"Hi Ms. Petersen, my name is Gary Willis and I am a salesperson for the ABC Company. The ABC company is*
>
> **1.**
> **2.**
> **3.**
>
> *This is what we do. Executives like yourself are asking us all the time . . .*
>
> **1.**
> **2.**
> **3.**
>
> *These are some of the questions we hear. If these are some of the issues you face, please feel free to call me at . . ."*

Companies that use this 30-second speech format have documented a two to three times increase in their callback ratio when they use a good 30-second speech. Why? Because they focus on WIIFM questions, which interest the prospect, since they have questions they want answers to, so they call back or take the call the next time the salesperson calls because they have a need or they know what issue will be discussed and they will not have to listen to a sales pitch . . . You get the point. Use 30-second speeches on the telephone.

- E-mail 30-second speeches work very well. Just keep the focus on the prospect, and remember to Summarize and Flip.
- Keep with the I–We–You perspectives. Start with I, then go to We, then finish up with You. When you go from Element 2 to Element 3, you cross the Your Bridge. Once

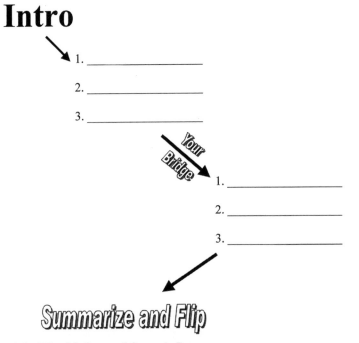

Figure 4-2. The 30-Second Speech Format.

you cross the Your Bridge, use only you and we, but never I unless you are paraphrasing in a WIIFM question.
- In this book, we are asking you to go Intro–3–3–Summarize and Flip. In the real world, you may go Intro–2–2– Summarize and Flip, or Intro–2–3–Summarize and Flip. Of course, you never want to go Intro–3–1–Summarize and Flip, since that puts the attention on you and not on the prospect.

Write your 30-second speech right now.

Bad Example—

Hello Ms. Smith.

My name is John Jones, and I am the Western Region Business Development Manager for the ABC Company, part of the XYZ family of Companies.

We are the largest company in the world that provides services for the wholesale industry that we believe are best of breed. We have been in business for 22 years and we have over 200 customers. If this sounds interesting to you, please call me back at 800-555-5555 and I can provide you with information about us that I am sure you will be interested in.

Good Example—

Hello Ms. Smith.

My name is John Jones, and I am with the ABC Company.

We are the largest company in the world that provides outsourcing services for the wholesale industry. We have been in business for 22 years, and we have over 200 customers, like the DEF and GHI Companies.

Executives like yourself ask us all the time,

"Is there a way to lower my overall cost of wholesale services?"

Or,

"How can I get my products to market faster using outside services?"

Or they ask,

"Are the risks of outsourcing finally low enough to consider outsourcing as a viable alternative in today's market?"

These are questions we hear all the time, and if they are of interest to you, please call me back at 800-555-5555, and we can provide you with further information or answer any questions you may have.

Figure 4-3. Good and bad examples of a 30-second speech

The 30-second speech is the tool that gives you a process by which you communicate during the prospecting part of selling. It supplies you with the confidence to give a prospect an overview of what you do and what's in it for them powerfully and concisely. It will allow you to have many different options for whatever language you need to speak and for any situation. Finally, it has the salesperson focusing on the prospect; this is what the prospect wants, and a ProActive sales person obliges. Use, practice, and perfect the 30-second speech. Make it your own, and watch the results.

Questions, Questions, Questions

The Initial Interest phase of the buy/sell process cannot be complete without a discussion on questions. The Law of Questions says an executive will agree to meet with you only because that executive has a question. It is up to the ProActive salesperson to ask questions to get the prospect's issues on the table so a discussion can take place. This is very important.

Sales management spends a great deal of time training their salespeople on product knowledge so that when they get in front of a prospect, usually a manager, they can spew out what they know. There are even names for this phenomena: Spray and Pray, Show up and Throw up, or Technicolor Yawn. Reactive salespeople disgorge product knowledge and do it with enthusiasm. They have PowerPoint slides, handouts, and brochures, all in the name of "educating" the customer. This is great. There will be a time when education is important, but ProActive salespeople know that great questions are not just something they think of at the spur of the moment. Like anything else, they need to be practiced.

Practice great questions. How? Be the customer.

When you are doing your homework, put yourself in the customer's chair. Physically move across your desk and into a "customer chair" if you have to. Ask yourself, "If I was the customer, what would be important to me right now? What is keeping me awake at night?" If you were the prospect, would you really be asking yourself, "How would I use your product or service?" They don't even know about your product or service. They do not care at the moment. It's all about them.

Questions will win the day, and you need to have done your homework to really think, "What questions are on my prospect's mind?" You need to write them down and have a discussion with your boss or with another sales associate on the questions you are going to ask. Practicing great questions will give you an advantage and stop you from executing the "Show up and Throw up" sales model when you are on the call.

The Columbo Sales Person: Asking Great Questions

A ProActive sales manager relays the following story.

Early in my career, I was promoted from sales representative to National Accounts Manager. My job was to oversee three major accounts and work with the local salesperson at each geographic location to make sure we had a coordinated effort with these major accounts. It was a big promotion for me, and obviously a reward for my previous sales success.

One of my accounts had offices in about eight major cities, so I had to deal with eight individual territory salespeople to make sure we had a consistent face to present to this customer. Well, in one location, Detroit, we had a pretty big division that was about to make a major purchase. Our salesperson assigned to the account, Dennis, was not anyone whom I would emulate. For one thing, he made his mark with small accounts. He sold a lot of "Mom and Pop" shops, but really did not have much experience with major accounts.

He really didn't dress professionally either. His suits were usually wrinkled, and although he was not sloppy, he did not project the kind of image I thought a person with our company should. I did not think he was the right salesperson for this sale and was considering taking him off the account. The fact that he had been the company's number one salesperson for 2 years in a row put an interesting twist into the mix. I could have him taken off the account, but that would not have been the right move at this time, so I decided to try and make it work.

We went on our first sales call together at the account. The call was going well, and I was letting Dennis do all the selling. Halfway through the meeting, however, Dennis was starting to drive me crazy.

The senior person in the room was asking questions, and Dennis was not answering them. The senior person would ask, "So what can your system do to solve this one particular problem?" The answer was obvious. We could do what the executive wanted to do, and do it very well. Dennis's response would be, "That's a good question. Why would you want to do that?" or, "That's a good question. How would you want the system to handle that?" It was driving me nuts. Finally, after about 10 minutes into this questioning session, I decided to get involved. After all, it was my right as the national account manager.

> *"Mr. Smith, we can do that, and we do that this way."*
>
> *"Mr. Smith, we have done that for many clients, and we*
>
> *can do that for you."*
>
> *"Mr. Smith, that's a good question. The answer is, yes, we*
>
> *can."*

I thought I was brilliant, as usual. We finished up the call, and as we were driving away, I asked Dennis, Mr. Number One in sales, Mr. Questions but no answers, Mr. Columbo (like the TV show, "I just have one more question"), what was he doing? Why, when asked a question by the senior person in the room, did he not show how we could address it?

He turned to me very calmly and said, "What makes you think he wanted an answer? Usually, I find that when they ask a question, they have an answer in mind. I always figured that if I could get them to answer their own question, they take ownership of my solution, and I usually get the sale."

It flashed across my mind that Dennis was right. I needed to put away my ego. I learned a great lesson that day. Ask great questions, have the customer figure out the answer to how you can help them, have ownership transfer, and you win. You do this by asking great questions, not by having great answers.

The prospecting call has three goals: the Introduction, the Middle, and the End. Goal 1 has been covered with the 30-second speech.

Goal 2: Introduce Your Product/Service— The Middle

In this part of the call you tell the prospect about your product/service, and your company gives you enough information to reach this goal. *Feature/Benefit* statements are the rule, and this part of the call follows three rules:

1. Always follow a feature with a benefit—What is in it for them.
2. Use multimedia and multiple formats to convey your message and to keep the introduction alive. It can be PowerPoint slides, flip charts, brochures, testimonials, or catalogs.
3. Keep the customers involved. The more they are involved with the introduction, the more they will get excited.

Goal 3: Do We Continue on Through a Buy/Sell Process?—The End

The purpose of Goal 3 is to end with you in control. It is time for a tool that lets you end every meeting professionally, ProActively, and with you in control.

Tool	**Summarize, Bridge, and Pull**Tool

Determining whether you want to continue on through a buy/sell process is the third goal of the Initiate sales call. The 30-second speech is how you start a call and address the first goal. A Summarize, Bridge, and PullTool (SBP) is how you end every call and address the last goal. *Every* call has to end with an SBP. Here is an example of an SBP:

> *"Well Mr. Grega, it sounds like we accomplished a lot*
>
> *today. You said you wanted to increase your revenue by*

getting your products through the development cycle 20
percent faster than they are taking today, increase the flexi-
bility you have in your packaging, and lower your overall
engineering costs by 10 percent, and we discussed how we
might be able to help. Would you agree?"

"Yes, I would. It has been a good meeting."

"Great. So a good next step should be where we both sit
down, we really learn more about what you want to accom-
plish, and you learn more about what we do. At that point,
you will be in a perfect position to determine whether we
should go any further with this conversation. Does that
sound good to you?"

This is a well executed SBP. You need to take it apart to see
the structure and then build it back up. A well executed SBP has
three parts:

1. You/I

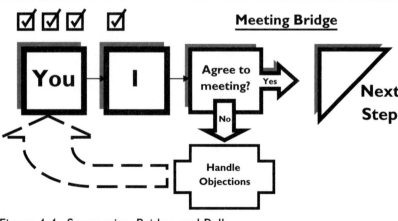

Figure 4-4. Summarize, Bridge, and Pull

2. Meeting Bridge

3. Next Step

You/I

This is where you summarize the discussion you just had, making sure you put the prospect's position first. Never put I first; it is a buy/sell cycle, not the other way around. Start with an introductory statement, and then go right for a "You position" statement.

INTRO STATEMENT

"Well Mr. Grega, it sounds like we accomplished a lot today.
    You: *You said you wanted to increase your revenue through getting your products through the development cycle by 20 percent, as well as increase the flexibility you have in your packaging, as well as lowering your overall engineering costs by 10 percent.*
    I: *We discussed how we might be able to help."*

Meeting Bridge

Here the salesperson prepares the prospect to go across the bridge with him or her. This is not losing control because you are the one proposing the bridge. Ask the prospect if he or she is ready to go across a bridge. You must ask about the meeting, since asking about You or I is one dimensional, and asking about the meeting is inclusive.

MEETING BRIDGE

"Would you agree we have had a good conversation?"
    "Would you agree we have had a good meeting?"
    "Yes, I would. It has been a very good meeting."

The buyer usually agrees because it is a summation of the conversation that just took place. You want him or her to agree that he or she had a good meeting; do not ask for agreement of the issues. They are agreeing that they said this, you said that, and it sounds pretty good right now. The prospect agrees to this because he or she was in the same conversation you were in, and you both have the same perspective of the meeting. The prospect must agree.

In some cases they may not, and you will uncover an objection that you need to deal with. It is better to uncover an objection early in the sale than to let it drag on to the end and become larger than life.

Next Step

This is when you propose the next step in the buy/sell process.

NEXT STEP

"Great. So a good next step should be where we both sit down, we really learn more about what you want to accomplish, and you learn more about what we do. At that point, you will be in a perfect position to determine whether we should go any further with this conversation. Does that sound good to you?"

In most cases, the prospect agrees since it is a natural next step in the process. You have completed an SBP and are in control of this sales call and this deal.

An SBP must be done after every meeting, after every conversation. It is very easy to lose control of a deal. It can happen in a split second, usually at the end of a meeting, when a prospect takes over and sends the deal in a different direction than you want it to go. You think it is just a detour, but it's not; it is a battle for control. An SBP is a tool to be used at the end of every sales call to keep control every step of the way.

Prospects want to be led, so you must be the one who does the leading. In role plays we do in our training seminars, we have salespeople take on the buyer's role. At the end of every role play scenario, we ask the salespeople who acted the parts of the buyers what they thought of the role plays. You can consistently depend on the salesperson who is in the role of the buyer to say something like:

"The things I noticed the most were the beginning and the end. If the role play started out with a 30-second speech, I felt good, like I knew what the agenda was and what the purpose of the meeting was. When the role-play ended with a Summarize, Bridge, and Pull, I felt like we were working together and it was a logical next step.

When there was no 30-second speech, I was busy thinking what am I here for, what is the point, what is the agenda, and what is the context of this conversation? I was thinking these things rather than listening to the salesperson. I wanted to know what the purpose of the meeting was, and we never really got to it. I got more and more annoyed during the call because I did not know the purpose of the call. I was not really listening to the sales pitch.

Worse, though, was when there was no Summarize, Bridge, and Pull. I ended up telling the salesperson what to do next, and I lost confidence in him. I felt he did not know what to do next, so I proposed a next step, and I usually proposed a next step without me in it, since I was not needed, and I could delegate it to other people on my staff. It was not important for me to be involved, and I could delegate this sale. By the way, the salespeople were happy to take my reference and delegation down a level too. They assumed it was a way to get into the organization, do some work, and then get back to me. Trust me, I was not going to let them get back in.

On your next sales call, write out how you want it to end.

OK, it sounds like we have had a good meeting.

YOU said you want to:

1. _____

2. _____

3. _____

and I have said that our company can

1. _____

So it sounds like we have had a good meeting,

would you **Agree**?

- Yes answer – Great, so a good **Next step** should be:

  _____

- No answer – So what do we need to cover that has not been addressed?

  _____

Figure 4-5. An SBP exercise

Again, the ones who worked each step of the Summarize, Bridge, and Pull are the ones I felt very comfortable with, who made me feel I was important in the process, and I really wanted to work with them on a next step."

Summarize, Bridge, and Pull is a way to make sure you are in control at the end of the meeting. Too often, salespeople leave a sales meeting thinking they are in control, when in actuality, someone else is pulling the strings. Typical mistakes salespeople make at the end of a sales call are:

- Ask the prospect what to do next. This is the classic case of a salesperson not being prepared with a next step. The salesperson thinks that if he does what the prospect tells him to do, then at the end, the prospect will give him the order. This is sales at its reactionary worst.
- Follow the prospect's requested next step. Being led by someone else is another classic sales mistake. The Law of Sales Control says the buyer is always neutral. If you are not controlling the sales process, someone else is, and usually that someone else does not have your best interest in mind.
- Do what the prospect asks you to do. This is similar to the preceding scenario, but here the prospect has detailed his or her entire buy process, usually a formal one, and a salesperson believes if he or she can follow the prospect's process better than anyone else, he or she will win the deal. This thinking is wrong because it is not their process to begin with, and will not be their process in the end. The salesperson who put the process together will own the deal.

   In many cases, prospects can make you feel like they are working with you on their process, so you feel you have a leg up. You have to believe they are making everyone feel that way.
- Try an SBP, then do what the prospect wants. A salesperson tries an SBP, and the buyer says he or she agrees, but

would rather do something else. Then the salesperson agrees to do what the prospect wants to do and leaves the proposed next step hanging.

> *"Well Mr. Grega, it sounds like we accomplished a lot today. You said you wanted to increase your revenue by getting your products through the development cycle by 20 percent, increase the flexibility you have in your packaging, and lower your overall engineering costs by 10 percent, and we discussed how we might be able to help, would you agree?"*
>
> *"Yes, I would. It has been a very good meeting."*
>
> *"Great. So a good next step should be where we both sit down, we really learn more about what you want to accomplish, and you learn more about what we do. At that point, you will be in a perfect position to determine whether we should go any further with this conversation. Does that sound good to you?"*
>
> *"That sounds good, but first I want you to talk with Bob and Mary (two managers, Spaniards of course.)"*

At this point the salesperson has a choice. He or she can agree with the prospect and go talk to Bob and Mary. In some cases, the salesperson is delighted to go talk to Bob and Mary because he or she now has a reference.

> *"Hi Bob, Mr. Grega, your boss, told me to call you . . ."*

This is quite a weapon, except it is useless because the prospect is now in control of the sale. Your tactic should be to agree with the prospect, and then gain control back.

> *"Yes, that sounds good. I will have a discussion with Bob and Mary by the end of the week. Let's then get back together, discuss the findings of that conversation, and then you and I can decide whether we should go*

*any further, since there is no way I am leaving this
meeting with you in control."* (You may want to
leave off the last bit and just think it, not say it.)

- Summarize and Pull with no Bridge. This is all salesperson and no prospect involvement—an easy trap to fall
  in, and can ruin a sale.

    *"Well Mr. Grega, it sounds like we accomplished a lot
    today. You said you wanted to increase your revenue by
    getting your products through the development cycle by
    20 percent, increase the flexibility you have in your
    packaging, and lower your overall engineering costs by
    10 percent, and we discussed how we might be able to
    help (no Bridge), so I think a good next step should be
    where . . .*

A Bridge is always needed. You must walk hand in hand
with the prospect across the Bridge. Going across first, then
yelling to the prospect to come along after you are already
across, is not a mutual sales process, and the prospect will feel
he or she "getting sold to." You must have a Bridge phrase:

> *"Would you agree?"*
> *"Does this sound about right?"*
> *"Is this what you thought we covered today?"*
> *"Are we of the same opinion on this?"*
> *"Do you concur?"*

Use what seems natural, but do use a Bridge. This is a mutual buy/sell process, and you must always Bridge to a Next
Step, not just go across the Bridge yourself and hope the prospect follows you.

Once you have mastered Summarize, Bridge, and Pull,
there is one more advanced step you may want to learn. It is
called Slaying the Dragons.

The You part of the SBP should be focused on them, natu-
rally. The advanced part of SBP says to remind the prospect why

they have these issues, these needs. There are Dragons driving these needs, and it is in the best interest of the ProActive salesperson to anchor these Dragons in their solution.

> *"Well Mr. Grega, it sounds like we accomplished a lot today. You said you wanted to increase your revenue by getting your products through the development cycle 20 percent faster than they are taking today because that is what is keeping you from getting earlier lifecycle profits (Dragon). You also want to increase the flexibility you have in your packaging because you have identified that varying your packaging options can increase your sales by an additional 15 percent (Dragon) and lower your overall engineering costs by 10 percent, which you have identified as one of the top initiatives your company has at this time (Dragon). We have also discussed how we might be able to help. Would you agree?*
>
> *"Yes, I would. It has been a good meeting."*
>
> *"Great. So a good next step should be where we both sit down and we really learn more about what you want to accomplish, and you learn more about what we do. At that point you will be in a perfect position to determine whether we should go any further with this conversation. Does that sound good to you?"*

Dragons are the pain points, the mission critical factors, and the real reasons why they are talking to you. By inserting these Dragons into your SBP, you will tailor the ending of the meeting to what is really in it for them, and stay in control of the sale.

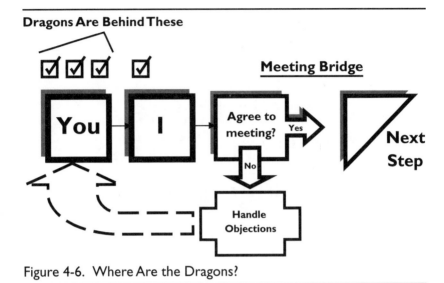

Figure 4-6. Where Are the Dragons?

Summarize, Bridge, and Pull is a powerful tool in the sales-person's repertoire. You will get to a point where you will feel strange if you do not use an SBP in a meeting. That will be a good sign, since without a SBP, control of the sales process is up for grabs. Be good, be ProActive, and use the SBP to stay in control of every meeting and every sale.

You are now proficient in using prospecting tools. Do it right, and SBP to the buyer's next step in the buyer's process, which is Education. For the ProActive salesperson, it is Educate.

Chapter 5

Educate the Customer Using Two-Way Learning

Salespeople and sales managers have varied viewpoints on what sales education is. Here's what sales education is not:

- *Telling the prospect all about you*
- *Telling the prospect the features of your product/service. This would be a regurgitation of product knowledge—something every salesperson wants to do, but really needs to do less*
- *Spewing out a standard sales presentation*
- *A demonstration of a product or service*
- *A one-way conversation about your product/service and what it can do for the customer*
- *A proposal*
- *Marketing literature delivered in e-mail, on the Web, in mail, or in person*
- *A contract*

Here is what ProActive sales education is.

THE LAW OF PROACTIVE SALES EDUCATION

Sales Education is where the salesperson or team finds out the real needs and motivation of the prospective customer, determines whether there is a mutual fit, and then proceeds to determine with the prospect why the customer should make a decision to change.

Look at this in three parts.

1. *Find out the real needs and motivation of the prospective customer.* This *must* be done first. The philosophy of the salesperson or sales team must be to find out what is really driving a need, and what is the real motivation behind this need. What are the dragons? The question of course is, if this is true, if a salesperson must find the driving need, why are so many slide presentations reactive, starting off with facts and figures about your company and its products/services?

2. *Determine whether there is a mutual fit.* The goal of sales education is not to convince someone to buy something from you; that would be a very one-dimensional approach. The real purpose of sales education is for the seller and the buyer mutually to agree on doing something. This implies that both the buyer and the seller must be informed, and it definitely means that the seller must know about the buyer's needs and motivation before he or she can start informing the buyer on what he or she is offering. The salesperson or team must therefore do their homework *before* they can start to educate the prospective buyer on the features and benefits of what the seller is offering.

3. *Determine with the prospect why he or she should make a decision to change.* The purpose is to have the customer determine with the salesperson (together so that there is a transfer of ownership) whether the prospect should make a decision for change. The ProActive salesperson understands that a salesperson is trying to sell something. Buyers, however, are not really buying something; they are changing something. They want or need to change. Most people don't like to change. They will make a purchase, do something different, reengineer, or develop something to invoke this needed change. You are hoping they make a purchase, and they purchase your good/service to satisfy this need for change. Great, but do not lose sight of the buyer's perspective. Selling them something is very one-dimensional. They want or need to change, and what you are offering is a vehicle to assist or satisfy their need. This should be a mutual win–win transaction.

The bottom line is that you are not selling something to someone. Think like a buyer, be ProActive, and understand his or her need for change. Help them with it, and create a mutual win–win. For successful salespeople this definition of sales education is second nature.

After all the training and experience you have had, you probably do a good job of sales education right now. You are now going to be adding some tools to your toolbox so you can be better at it. These tools should be used during sales education to help you stay in control:

- Feature/Benefit/Value Selling^{Tool}
- ProActive sales presentations
- SalesMap^{Tool}

Tool   **Feature/Benefit/Value Selling^{Tool}**

During the sales education process, ProActive sales people subscribe to the rule of Feature/Benefit/Value (FBV) selling, since this is the selling language of calling high. It slays dragons. FBV states that for every feature you toss out to the prospect, you must a have a benefit and a value for the buyer, a WIIFM.

> *"We have a new level of premium service (feature), and*
>
> *what this means to you is 20 to 30 percent quicker response*
>
> *to your problems (benefit), saving you up to 10 percent of*
>
> *your current costs (value)."*
>
> *"Our new product is 20 percent faster, which means up to*
>
> *35 percent less time your people will be spending waiting*
>
> *for the machine to get started, saving you 10 percent over-*
>
> *all in manufacturing costs this year."*
>
> *"By allowing you access to this new service, you will be*
>
> *able to get your product to market in 1/3 of the time, and*
>
> *with 10 percent less risk."*

FBV differs from Feature/Benefit selling since it allows the salesperson to sell effectively to the top two levels of the organization, vice presidents and CEOs. Feature/Benefit is selling what lower level managers want to hear. When talking to managers, there is no need for any value statements, since they are not interested in value. FBV allows you and upper level management to share in the presentation. Keep the focus on them, since you are talking about their value and their WIIFM.

You need to stop any one-way sales education meetings, the ones that are all about you, and start developing sales strategies for how to conduct a sales education call that has mutual benefit. To do that, you need to provide value to the prospect. Use FBV statements to gain a competitive advantage.

In addition, FBV selling helps ProActively induce transfer of ownership, since you are working with the prospect to determine the real worth of the solution you are offering. FBV is hard to apply in every sales call, but when you do use this tool, you and the prospect are on the same page and end up working hard together, since you both have WIIFM interests and are both interested in satisfying the customer's dragons.

Evaluate your current sales presentations. Are they one way, requiring that the prospect sits and listens to you, the "I know it is only 35 slides, but I can get through them in a hurry" selling presentation disasters? The problem is you do not think they are a disaster, but the Russians and Greeks always do.

Turn Sales Education into ProActive Sales Presentations

Most companies have their own philosophies on sales presentations. Some prefer to do demonstrations; others would rather stick to PowerPoint slides or "decks," and still others would rather review technical or marketing literature. Style and company philosophies can be very important in the sales education process when delivering product/service features and benefits.

What is just as critical as features and benefits in the sales presentations are the tactics of the sales presentation. You need to look at ways you can improve your sales education tactics and make your sales presentations ProActive.

The goal of sales education is to create a two-way flow of information. First, a ProActive salesperson must set the stage for the attainment of this goal. Reactive salespeople typically walk into the meeting room, take out their laptop computers, plug them into a computer projection system, turn off the lights, and start with a 30-plus slide presentation. The presentation lasts 20 to 40 minutes, the computer goes off, the lights come on, and the salesperson asks, "Are there any questions?" This is not a two-way education meeting. What really happens is that the salesperson begins with the lights on, discusses an agenda for 5 minutes, dives into the presentation, answers a few questions that are all about the product or service presented, then turns on the lights at the end.

The phone sales presentation follows the same format. After a good 30-second speech, the agenda is set, and the prospect starts to talk. As soon as the prospect begins talking, the salesperson goes into answer mode, trying to formulate answers so that as soon as there is a pause in the discussion, he or she can jump in and start "selling."

It is time to give your sales education process an overhaul and make it effective in terms of the prospect. The delivery tactics of sales presentations need to be refined. It does not matter if *you* think that yours is good; what matters is whether it good from the prospect's point of view. These ProActive prospect-focused tactics are what you need work on, because it is all about them.

There are three parts of a sales presentation that need to be addressed to make a sales education presentation ProActive.

1. The Beginning: Setting the Stage
2. The Middle: Them Then Us Presentations
3. The Ending: The Mutual Agreement to a Next Step

Note that these parts are similar to the three parts of generating Initial Interest.

Part 1: The Beginning—Setting the Stage

The beginning of every sales call, of every sales presentation, is crucial. It sets the stage for the entire meeting, informs everyone of the agenda, and gets all the important issues on the table, especially the ones from the prospect that have occurred since the last meeting that the salesperson knows nothing about.

Too many things happen in between sales calls, and there are too many times sales people have stopped at mid-meeting to be told by the meeting attendee leader,

> *"Gayle, this is good, but some things have changed that*
>
> *you need to know about before you continue."*

Unless you set the stage properly, the prospect most likely won't speak up before the meeting starts. Instead of addressing his current concerns, you will end up wasting half the meeting on topics that are now of no interest to him.

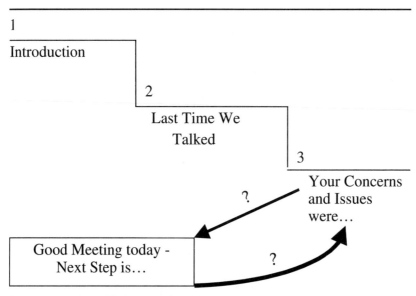

Figure 5-1. The 30-Second Speech for Sales Call #2 and Beyond

To start a meeting or a presentation successfully, you should use the 30-second speech. Every meeting or presentation, not just a prospecting call, must start out with a 30-second speech. The 30-second speech format never changes, Introduction/3/3/Summarize and Flip. What changes for every sales call and presentation after the first one are the bullets you use in the 30-second speech. Look at the differences:

30-Second Speech	*First Speech*	*All Other Sales Calls*
Opening	Introduction	Introduction
Second Element	About Us	Last Time we talked
Third Element	About Them	Your Concerns and Issues were . . .
Closing	Summarize and Flip	Good Meeting Today— Next Step is . . . then Flip back to Concerns and Issues

The Second, Third, and Closing elements change to fit the circumstance of the meeting. The basic structure you learned in the last chapter does not change, so the tool you learned to prospect effectively is now the same tool you can leverage on every sales call.

In the role plays that are used in our ProActive Sales training seminars, top salespeople get a chance to use and listen to 30-second speeches. Three conclusions always come out of these role plays:

1. Good 30-second speeches always come across very well, regardless of how the salesperson believes it was delivered.

2. Top salespeople are doing something similar to 30-second speeches already, but not as powerful and leverageable. When they practice and get comfortable with it, they are very good at it and incorporate it into their sales toolbox.

3. When the salesperson is the buyer in the role plays scenarios, he or she actually likes the 30-second speech for the second and beyond format better, since it proposes a next step before the meeting begins. If the prospect agrees, then all the salesperson has to do is execute on the agenda of the meeting and not have to worry about taking control at the end, since it already has been established what the next step is. Even if, during the meeting, the next step needs to change, the salesperson has created a leveraged situation so at the end of the meeting he or she can propose a next step already outlined and agreed to at the beginning of the meeting. He or she can say,

> *"It seems we have had a good meeting. We agreed earlier that if today's meeting went well, our next step was going to be xxx. It now seems you have stated a desire to learn more about our services offering, and we need to get you that information before we proceed, do we agree? Great, so our next step now should be . . ."*

An SBP has been inserted here as well, but since an agenda and next step were established at the beginning of the meeting with the 30-second speech, the salesperson has tools that are still flexible enough to control the next step of the sales process even though the prospect has changed the meeting agenda. The opportunity for the salesperson to lose control of the sales process here is very high, but with the 30-second speech setting up every meeting and establishing the next step from the start, and using an SBP at the end, the salesperson has the tools required to stay in control.

Use the 30-second speech to begin every sales call. The beginning of a sales presentation is all about setting the agenda and setting the control and tempo of the meeting. A 30-second speech opening, followed by discussing or reviewing what was said in the 30-second speech, is the most powerful way to begin a sales call or presentation, either in person or over the phone. The beginning conversation can last a few minutes, or, if you hit the prospect's hot button, up to half of the entire meeting. The 30-second speech agenda comes across to the prospect as a professional setting of the meeting agenda and gives you overall control of the meeting.

Part 2: The Middle—Them Then Us Presentations

The middle part of the sales presentation is really the content part of the meeting. It is the discussion of features, benefits, and the value your products and services are going to be delivering, and you are highlighting why the prospect should buy from you. For this middle part of sales presentations to be effective and ProActive, it must be interesting to the prospect. How do you prepare for a sales presentation so it is effective, ProActive, and really interesting to the prospect? Just follow the Muhammad Ali School of Presentations format.

Muhammad Ali, the great boxer, adopted a theory of boxing he used late in his career. In the twilight of his boxing career he knew he was fighting men who were stronger, younger, and faster than he was, and if he went toe-to-toe with them in the boxing ring, his odds of winning were low. Aware that he was aging, he developed a school of thought that if his job was to win the fight, the most likely way he was going to win was not by a knockout but by a decision of the boxing judges. He believed that boxing judges were most impressionable in the first

30 seconds and the last 30 seconds of every round. In the middle of a round, he would save his strength, cover up, and do the rope-a-dope. (This is a boxing term Muhammad invented for a ploy whereby he would just lie on the ropes of the boxing ring and let his opponent punch him while he covered up, letting his opponent get tired while he rested.) This gave him the strength for the last 30 seconds of the round to make a lasting impression on the judges.

Presentations are very similar. The opening and closing discussions of any presentation are the most important; they are the controlling parts of the sales meeting. The middle of the meeting, the product and service discussion, is the rope-a-dope.

The beginning and end of a presentation are the tactical areas to focus on to maintain control. The middle is useful, and it contains the most information, but it's not how you gain and stay in control. You use the middle of the presentation to discuss what you are selling and to get input from the prospect.

The middle of the presentation or sales education part of the sales call must be organized in a Them-Then-Us format. This is very important from prospect's standpoints because the sales presentation should be all about them. The format of the middle of the sales call/presentation needs to be:

1. Them
2. Us
3. Them

Don't use Map Presentations. They are ineffective, since they are in Us–Them–Us format.

The Map Presentation

A Map presentation is one in which the salesperson delivers a presentation, usually in PowerPoint, to a room of prospects. The first slide is the title slide with the salesperson's company and logo information. The second and third slides are all about the company history and performance. At about the third or fourth slide, a picture of a map or globe comes up, and there are some stars or dots that highlight where the selling organization has offices or factories located around the world. It is a very attractive slide and looks impressive.

The question is, Do you really think the prospect cares where your offices around the world are right now? Why would you put this map slide in the front of your presentation? Are you trying to impress the customer?

"I am trying to establish credibility."

Stop and think. If you weren't credible, you would not be in there giving a presentation. The only reason prospects, especially vice presidents, agree to a meeting is because they have a question to ask. They do not want to see a map with your locations on it. They want to talk—about themselves. Remember: It is all about them.

The middle of the presentation must focus on them, so start with talking about them, and end with talking about them. In the middle, you can talk about you. Have your first few slides of this middle part of the presentation be based on your homework or on leading questions that start them to talk. You want at least the first 20 percent of the meeting to be about them. Your slides or presentation material should stimulate thought and get them involved.

Then there should be a natural lead into what you do and how they can apply what you do to the conversation you just had about them. No one, except for a few diehard Spaniards, wants to sit through a presentation and listen to what you have to say about you for longer than 5 to 10 minutes at a time. This goes back to the value proposition discussed in Chapter 1. No one cares about your value proposition. They care about their own value proposition and how they can become more competitive. The middle of your presentation should reflect this interest.

End the middle part of the presentation with what the information about you means to them. Use Feature/Benefit and Feature/Benefit/Value statements to summarize your points, and then stimulate their thinking by asking questions about what this means to them or how they would use this.

Part 3: The Ending—The Mutual Agreement to a Next Step

Now it is time for the Ending. You have done a great job in getting the prospect involved in the beginning, getting issues out, and tailoring the middle of your presentation so he or she "gets it." You delivered your story and related it to the discussion you mutually had in the beginning. It is now time to end the presentation and keep the sales process going.

The Ending is a way for you to summarize the meeting, gain agreement, and then offer a next step. In other words, you need to Summarize, Bridge, and Pull to finish a presentation.

Your Ending can be very formal and last 20 minutes or so, based on the complexity of the issues or the risk involved in a next step, or it could take 5 minutes, based on the simplicity of moving forward. The Ending of a presentation follows three rules.

1. Follow the format of an SBP.
2. Keep prospects involved by having them do an SBP with your guidance.
3. Create a **SalesMap**^{Tool}

To follow the format of an SBP, you should:

- Summarize the meeting.
- Gain agreement.
- Propose a next step.

During the summarize part you should summarize the meeting, staying focused on the prospect's solution, not on what you are offering. A 3:1 ratio of what they have said they desire to what you are offering is a good way to remember how much you should focus and talk about the prospect during the summary.

The Bridge is a way to get them to discuss the presentation itself, the pros and the cons, and to have them air their true feelings about your presentation, as well as offer up any final objections (see Figs. 4.1 and 4.2).

Pulling to the next step includes the final summary and offering up the next step in the buy/sell process so that you stay in control of the meeting. The ending of the ProActive sales presentation must be interactive and have the prospect involved, so much so that it will feel like the prospects are closing themselves. If you do it right, they really are closing themselves, with you in control.

The Customer Pen: Keep Them Involved

Many salespeople close a meeting with a customer pen. They have a Magic Marker or "Customer Pen" they bring out at the end of a meeting. To keep the prospect involved, they give the pen to the top-ranking executive in the meeting and ask, "Would you mind taking this pen, going to the board, and summarizing today's meeting so we can make sure we are all on the same page?"

What usually happens is that the executive gets up and goes to the board, or gives the pen to someone the executive trusts, and he or she goes to the board and starts to summarize the meeting. They start out slowly and usually need a little prompting, but after a minute or so they start to close themselves.

> *". . . and if we had this system, we then could use it on that*
>
> *new project that just got stuck last week in engineering . . ."*

The salesperson now transforms from being a musician in the orchestra during a concert to being the conductor, leading all the elements in one song rather than having different conversations and opinions going on at the same time and having to manage it all themselves. The Customer Pen also helps to transfer ownership, something that will be discussed in Chapter 7.

There are obvious comparisons between ProActive sales presentations and the old way:

Old Way	*ProActive Way*
• Tell them (*what you are going to say*).	• *Ask them* (what they want to discuss).
• Tell them.	• *Tell them, and ask* if they understand/what would they do if . . .
• Tell them (*what you have said*).	• *Ask them* (what you both have said, agree, then SBP).

Do you see the difference? The old way of sales presentations was very unidirectional. You spoke at the client, and he or she was supposed to listen. The ProActive way creates much more mutual involvement and is under the salesperson's control. ProActive sales presentations should accomplish the following:

- In the beginning, the salesperson is in control of the meeting and should involve the prospect. Ask the prospect what he or she wants to accomplish.
- The middle of the presentation should inform the prospect what you do and how it relates to the prospect's needs, which were stated in the beginning of the meeting. You both talk about what's in it for the prospect.
- Then the presentation should finish with an SBP and ask them if they want to go to a next step.

It is a simple, clean, and winning formula. Now, go and change those slides. Give a ProActive sales presentation, and educate your prospect in a ProActive manner. A few final tips on Sales Presentations:

- Map Presentations or Map Slides: Get rid of them; focus on the prospect instead.
- Magic Markers: This is probably the most powerful sales education tool—every sales person should have a set of multicolored magic markers in his or her briefcase. Otherwise, you are at the mercy of their supplies, for example, old semidried out green magic markers, which are

not very visually appealing or convincing. Use color, and a lot of it. It will keep your presentation in the prospect's mind longer, and make a competitive difference since most reactive salespeople are using that old green marker.

- For every feature you want to reinforce, write down the benefits and the value to the prospect, as well as the feature. WIIFT (What's in it for them) is the major theme.
- Use multiple mediums. A flip chart and a projector are more powerful than just using a projector. If you are going to use only a flip chart, use two, so you can make a point and reference your other point if you need to during the meeting.
- Keep the energy going. Ask, "What would you do with this?" type questions to keep the prospect involved. Do not let him or her listen to you speak for longer than 5 to 10 minutes at a time. The brain can only take so much of one-way communication before it shuts down. Salespeople may be having a great time and be really on a roll making a great point, but if the audience has turned off their brains, nothing is getting through. Stay with the 5- to 10-minute rule.
- Use analogies. Stories are great education tools. When you are making a point, use a story. It becomes a powerful anchor.
- Give them a simple worksheet to fill out. Give them a quiz. Ask for their opinions. In the middle of the presentation, a way of getting them involved is having them write something down, even if it is to write what they have just heard you say on a Post-it note. Having them write something down forces them to remember, and is also a great way for objections to come out, and for you to get them to share what is on their minds.

It's All About ME!

The prospect must be thought of in the introduction, in the middle, and at the end of a sales presentation, period. Practice by having some other salespeople or non-salespeople sit in and critique your next presentation. Have some office administrators sit in, and then let them tell you what they have heard. If they start to repeat all the things you have said about your offering, or even if they just keep the focus of the discussions on your product/features, you have done it wrong. If they start to state what they have heard and what it means to them, how they are going to use it, you have done it right.

It is hard to keep the focus of the conversation on them. There usually comes a time when the prospect wants to hear more, or a panic time when you are at a loss to answer a direct question the prospect is asking. The natural tendency is to go back to what you know best: product knowledge. This is the last thing you should feel you know the most about. Practice reference stories, asking other secondary questions, and Flips. It is about having comebacks and Flips for managers who want to keep the presentation at the *Feature/Function* (Spanish) level, not about the salesperson who has the most product knowledge and speaks the most fluent Spanish. Practice these tactics to get good at them. Winging it, or just saying whatever comes to your mind at the time, is a reactive and risky technique at best.

The best question that works at all three levels and makes sure you are focusing on the prospect during sales education, is the "so what" question.

> *"So what does that mean to you?"*
>
> *"So what would you do with this?"*
>
> *"So what else will you be doing when this is implemented?"*
>
> *"So what would stop you from going ahead with this?"*
>
> *"So what . . . ?"*

The "So what . . . ?" question is what the other people in the practice session should be asking you, and you should be asking yourself on every point you make. This ensures you have the prospect's best interest in mind and are ready for any objections.

Be ProActive, and learn how to get comfortable talking about them. They want to talk about themselves, and you should let them; you will sell more if you do.

The Danger in the Unspoken Feature

Here is a word of caution for ProActive salespeople: Salespeople, like everyone else, get bored saying the same thing over and over. What's worse, they assume that since they have said *it* for the last 200 meetings they have been in, that everyone knows *it*, and therefore *it* is a commodity. The unspoken feature ends up being your competitor's exclusive.

Too many deals have been lost by the prospect saying, "I didn't know you offered that as well," or the salesperson saying, "I told them that when we first met. It's not my fault they didn't remember." Yes, it is your fault.

There are hundreds of reasons why prospects should buy your product/service, but they end up focusing on just two or three, and usually it is a different two or three for every buyer. When you find what prospects want, you should repeat the feature you have that meets their need, and the benefit and the value it provides, over and over again. You have won deals because the prospect liked a key feature you offer and the benefits it provided. Your competitor has that same feature/benefit, something similar, or another feature/benefit that you do not have. Find out what is important to prospects, and then tell them over and over again. Get them to tell you over and over. Someone is talking about the unspoken feature, and it is usually that someone who gets the order.

`Tool`   The SalesMap^Tool: The Roadmap to the Deal

You and the prospect now have enough information from using the tactics you have just mastered during the sales education phase of selling. It is now time to finish the sales education phase, Summarize, Bridge, and Pull to the next step called Validate. Before doing that, you need one more tool, the SalesMap^Tool.

Most salespeople, at the end of the Educate step, feel confident about their chances. It is now that the deal can either be solidly entrenched in your camp, or can slip though your fingers. Salespeople often ask,

> *"How can I as a salesperson lead the prospect through the rest of the sale rather than feel like I am being led and being reactive? Is there a way to map out the rest of the buy/sales cycle and stay in control from this point forward?"*

There is in fact a map that identifies the steps that need to be taken by both prospect and seller, and how to have the prospect and seller agree on these steps while the salesperson stays in control. It's like an SBP but describes the rest of the buy/sell process to the prospect. It then allows the salesperson to take control of the rest of the process, not just a single step. It's called a **SalesMap**ᵀᵒᵒˡ.

Trip-Tik: A Personal Story

I was born and raised in Cleveland, Ohio. Every December, we would travel to Tampa, Florida for the holidays. All eight of us would get into the car, complain about who was sitting where, and head to Tampa.

Once on the road, the only people who knew where we were going were my mom, my dad, and the AAA (American Automobile Association). Why? Because every year my parents would get a series of maps from the AAA called a Trip-Tik. This Trip-Tik was a series of maps bound in a book that was customized for the member who was taking a trip by car. For us, our Trip-Tik would start in Cleveland, and at the bottom of the first page, would end in Columbus, Ohio. If you turned the page, it would then start at Columbus, and at the bottom of the second page would be Cincinnati. There were 20 to 25 pages in all, and it would finally end with the bottom of the last page in Tampa. This was great. Page one had Cleveland to Columbus; at the last page, you were somewhere in Florida near Tampa to Tampa. In between were all the roads and exits we had to take to get to Tampa. It highlighted the detours, hotels, restaurants, and even places where speed traps might have been set up by the state highway patrols. It basically detailed the route we should take to get to Tampa, and what we could expect along the way.

This was a fabulous tool. If we did not have a Trip-Tik we could all have piled in the car, started in Cleveland, and ended up in Houston, which is a great place, but not where we wanted to go.

The Trip-Tik was a mutual guide for us getting to our destination. We decided where we wanted to go, worked with our partners, who told us how to get there, and we followed their directions. The Pro-Active Selling SalesMap is a mutual guide for prospects to get to their destination, which is a choice. Prospects decide where they want to go, usually work with a single partner who is in control of the sale, and follow the sales team's directions because they have confidence in their ability and professionalism based on the completeness of a SalesMap.

These are two different journeys, but use the same effective tool.

Figure 5-2 is an example of a SalesMap. A SalesMap should be a document that is mutually worked on in the beginning, then referenced and updated at every opportunity.

The SalesMap is one of two tools discussed in *ProActive Selling* that everyone agrees has a tremendous amount of value, but it takes some work to develop and implement. Many salespeople agree with the idea of a SalesMap, but fail to implement it since it requires some planning and some effort to get good at. If you really want to control the sales process, you must use the tools, especially the SalesMap. It is the best way to control the sales process, because it requires mutual collaboration. It is tough to build a house without a blueprint; it's tougher to win a sale without a SalesMap.

You are on a roll. You have completed what has to be done in the Educate process to feel confident and really understand what prospects want. They understand what you do and the value they will get by buying from you, and you have covered all the bases. It's looking very good. It's time to Summarize, Bridge, and Pull to the next step in the process, Validate.

Before you go any further, however, you want to make sure you have a qualified deal. Things may look good right now, but a good salesperson needs to have a highly qualified deal. You need to qualify to a ProActive salesperson's measure, not just

Prospect Company: _____

Contact Name: _____

Initial Sales Call Date: _____/_____/_____

What are the steps we have taken together so far?

1. _____

2. _____

3. _____

What are the next buy/sell steps you want to take to make sure a decision is made?

Complete?

Yes   No

1. _____   ☐   ☐

2. _____   ☐   ☐

3. _____   ☐   ☐

4. _____   ☐   ☐

5. _____   ☐   ☐

Insert steps the prospect is going to be taking on their own.

Update this SalesMap after every sales call.

Figure 5-2. Sample SalesMap

some document you fill out and give to your boss to get a stamp of approval. Real qualification skills help you during the first two steps of the buy/sell process and during actual sales calls to make sure you are spending your valuable time wisely with this account. ProActive qualification skills are discussed next.

Chapter 6

Qualify: Not a Phase but a Process

You are now in control of your sale. You started off doing homework on the accounts you wanted to call on. You know where you should be spending your time, what information you should be gathering, when you should be prospecting your A-level customers, and you know what to say in your sales opening to capture their interest. You then have implemented some sales education tools to make sure the prospect really understands WIIFT. You have actually developed a SalesMap with the prospect, and he or she has agreed to work with you on it. You already have ideas on where to spend your commission from this deal, since you know you have a highly qualified deal, right? Let's find out.

How Salespeople and Sales Managers Should Spend Their Time

In Chapter 1, the phases of the buy/sell process were outlined, as well as the way in which a ProActive salesperson goes through these phases step by step to win a deal. You have already made it through the generating interest phase (Initiate), are now finishing up the Education step (Educate), and are heading for the Validation phase (Validate). Before you go any further in this sale, you have to make sure you have a qualified deal.

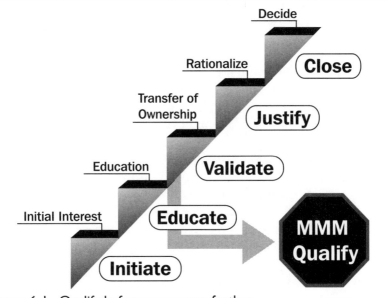

Figure 6-1. Qualify before you go any further.

This is of course speaking from a salesperson's point of view. Salespeople and sales managers ask all the time,

"How can I make sure I really have a qualified situation?"

The answer is you can never be sure. You will, however, be given some tools right now to make sure you can confidently and effectively qualify.

Qualifying Goals

The goal of qualifying is to give you a better than 50 percent chance of closing the sale. That is all qualification skills should do. By making sure you are working a qualified deal you will:

- Work on the deals you have a better than 50 percent chance of winning, so you can increase your close ratio.

- Close more deals by eliminating the maybes.
- Force prospects into a decision as to whether they really want to continue with this buy/sell evaluation at this time.
- Stop working the 0 to 50 percent probability deals. Why would you work on these deals anyway? You have a better chance of winning in Las Vegas than trying to close a deal at 30 percent probability.
- Increase the chances for success early in the deal. You have not expended too many resources on this deal yet, but now it is ramping up, and you will be spending time and energy with demonstrations, proposals, and the like. The better you qualify early in the process, the sooner you can make a decision if this is a deal you want to be spending time on.

It may be hard to believe, but it is better to get rid of unqualified deals and get out there and *prospect* (not an unpleasant word anymore now that you have your ProActive tools). Those *AB* and *AC* accounts are being closed without you. Getting rid of unqualified deals and prospecting some new opportunities makes good selling sense.

MMM: The Qualification Process

The ProActive Selling qualification process focuses on getting the qualification information from the prospect. To get information, you have to ask questions. To get good qualification information, you have to ask good questions.

Good qualification questions are centered on three probing areas, which are called the three Ms:

- Money
- Method
- Motivation

Qualification of a deal is a skill, and if it is mastered, it will affect a salesperson's success more than anything else. In the years that ProActive Selling has been around, it has been found that if a salesperson can master the MMM qualification questions, these questions will do more to affect a salesperson's income than any other tool in ProActive Selling. MMM has seven questions.

The Seven Questions

Did you ever wonder how you get to master great sales questions? You read books, watch sales videos, listen to sales training tapes, observe other top salespeople, and you try to pick up tips that will help you to sell more effectively. You know you have to ask great questions, but what are great questions? Great questions always seem to be on the sales training videotape, not in real life. In real life, you ask a question like:

"Do you have a budget for this project?"

In the sales training videotape, you hear the same question you are asking, but it comes out a little different.

"Mr. Lewis, given the benefits of the solution we are look-

ing at, what would the process of obtaining budgetary

funds be in your organization?"

Although this may seem like the same question, it isn't really. The seven qualifying questions will give you the ammunition you need to ask great qualification questions, starting with the first M, Money.

Money

Question 1: Money—What, Not Who

The first question addressed is money, the number one question to be answered. If the prospect does not have a way to pay for what you are offering, why would you be working on a particular deal? The prospect, without money or resources, may have you occupied for months and prevent you from working on sales opportunities with real potential.

There is one question for Money, but it is in two parts. First, however, every salesperson knows the real question he or she would like to ask concerning Money. All salespeople would love to look at the buyers they are talking to, especially Spanish ones, and point blank ask:

"Ms. Larsen, are you an important person in this process,

or do I have to go over your head to get a decision?"

You cannot ask this question, but don't you wish you really could? This question is the wrong question because it focuses in the wrong place. It asks *who*, which is a big mistake. As a ProActive salesperson, you need to be asking *what*. The two *what* questions you need to ask under Money are:

1. *"What is the process for obtaining a budget for a*

   decision like this?"

2. *"What is the process for making a decision?"*

These are the questions you ask under Money. Money focuses on the *what* questions. You want to focus on the *what* questions for the following reasons:

- *What* is a buyer's question—Buyers ask themselves *what* all the time.
  - "What should we do from here?"
  - "What is the process we need to go through to get Jack to sign off on this project?"
  - "What do you think we should do first?"
  - "What approvals do you think we are going to need to get this project approved?"
  - "What do we have to do to get more money if we exceed the current budget?"

What questions are the questions the buyers are asking themselves all day long. After your sales manager has drilled you on "Who is making the decision?" you go in to the prospect and ask a sales question like your boss has told you to do:

- "Who is buying our product/service?"
- "Who has the budget?"
- "Who is the person making the decision?"

The buyer, being unfamiliar with these question, looks around and says, "I am." You then think there is no way anyone would put this person in charge of anything, let alone a decision like this.

Of course you cannot say this, but you are certainly thinking it. You are also now stuck. This person has said he or she is in charge, and if you need to go around this person, you have a problem because that person has told you he or she is in charge. If you want to go see a higher level manager, a Russian for instance, you now have to figure out a stealthy way of doing it. Forget about *who;* ask *what.* The only question under Money is *what,* and the reason is:

- *What* is a process question, and companies work in processes—"What's the process for a budget?" not, "Do you have a budget?" It really doesn't matter if they have a budget or not. Budgets are fluid at a senior management level. If the value on the investment they are making for your solution is high enough, they will go get more budget money from someone or somewhere else. Vice presidents and C-level managers can find more budget, lower level managers can only spend what their superiors give them. You want to know the process of getting budget money, not what the budget is. If you work to their fixed budget, who is really in control?
- *What* encourages discussion and gets more information—*Who* questions limit the discussion to people. *What* questions focus the discussion on people, process, and

who has the power. You can gather more information with *what* questions.

- *Who* is a point answer—you can answer it with one name. *What* describes the process, giving you many points of reference and a look at the entire picture.
- *What* can include you; *who* cannot. You may want to know if prospects are including you in their buy process.
- *What* can be revisited at every call. A salesperson can ask about changes to the process and even suggest changes. It is tough to suggest changes while asking *who*.

Money questions are *overall* process questions. What is the overall process:

- To obtain funds?
- To make a decision within the organization?
- The committee is going to take in making a decision?

You get more bang for the buck with *what*.

Method

The first M, Money, has been addressed, and you now have some questions in your sales toolbox you can ask the prospect to determine whether you have a qualified deal. Method, the second M, focuses its questions on the buyer's *specific* process.

There are three questions that need to be answered in Method:

1. What is the Implementation Date?
2. What are the steps in the buy/sell process?
3. What are the Decision Criteria?

Tool	**Question 2: Implementation Date**Tool— **The Maybe Killer**

Nothing kills a sale like a maybe. Yes's are great; both you and the prospect win. No's are great also; they let you know you are doing something wrong, and you can fix it. It's the maybes that will kill you.

A maybe is the prospect's way of getting and maintaining control of the deal. The truth is that if the prospect is in control, the Law of Sales Control mentioned earlier states they are talking to someone else, and someone else is in control.

They don't get back to you in a timely manner. Meetings slip. It takes days for e-mails to be answered, if at all. You end up wondering if this sale is ever going to close. The answer is yes it will close, and it will close without you.

There is a name for this type of selling, by the way. This highly reactive, wait-by-the-phone-and-hope-the-call-will-come selling is called Funeral Selling.

FUNERAL SELLING

When you go to a funeral you usually go up to the bereaved at the end of the service and solemnly state,

> *"I'm so sorry. If there is anything I can do,*
>
> *please let me know."*

Change of scene. Go to the reactive salesperson on the phone leaving a voice message.

> *"If there is anything I can do to move this order*
>
> *along, please let me know."*

The words are the same in both cases; it is Funeral Selling—reactive selling at its worst.

It's time to be ProActive. It is time to qualify this deal to see if you are in control or not. The tool you are going to use to gain control back and destroy maybes is called the Implementation Date^Tool.

Salespeople have been taught to focus on the wrong date. Assume you are currently in a sale. You began the sale a little while ago, and you see the end of the buy/sell process coming up soon—that end date when the prospect is going to make a decision.

You know exactly what happens on that date. The prospect is going to sign the order, you get the order, you are happy, your boss is happy, and everybody wins.

You have the wrong date. The "Prospect expects to close date" is a seller's, not a prospect's, term. Prospects could care less when they sign an order. Signing an order is just getting the P.O. out of purchasing, part of a process. What prospects really care about is the Implementation Date.

"What date do you plan to start using or implementing

what we are talking about?"

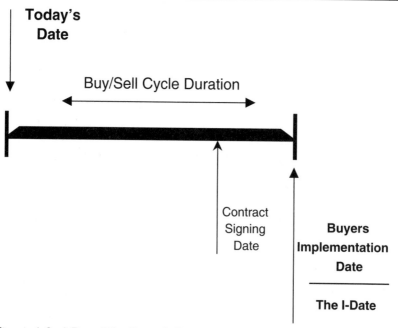

Figure 6-2. I-Date: The Buyer's Focus

"When do you want to have the solution up and running?"

"What date does the financial justification start from?"

The Implementation Date, or I-Date, is when prospects want their order on their desk or when they are going to start using what you are trying to sell them. It could be defined as the date they start making money from the investment you are offering, when can they load it on their computer, have it on their dock, or start to implement the benefits that you are offering. The date the contract is signed is secondary compared with the date they have what you are selling them in their possession so they can start doing their job. This is what the prospect cares about; they care about their Implementation Date.

I-DATES: DO YOU REALLY CARE?

- *When you bought the shoes, or when you had them on your feet and could wear them to that special event?*
- *When you paid for the vacation, or when you went on it?*
- *When you bought the big screen TV, or when you had it set up and started to watch it?*

Prospects place importance on I-Dates more than any other date in the buy/sell process for the following reasons:

- It is when they promised their boss something would change.
- It is when they have scheduled other activities to commence (kick-off meetings, training, launch of something else that coincides with your product being implemented).
- A customer is involved, or there is a customer timeline involved.

- A schedule must be met.
- The company or department will increase their risk if they do not acquire what you are selling them.
- There is a deadline for another project for which your item is on the critical path.
- There is political pressure on something that your good/ service is a part of.

There are a host of reasons that can tie what you are offering to an Implementation Date. Rest assured, your prospect has an I-Date. It is very important to know that an Implementation Date and that a Contract Close or Contract Sign date are different dates. They have to be since they are coming from two perspectives, the seller's and the prospect's. Each party is approaching this deal differently and has a different reason for this deal to conclude. The salesperson wants to know when the sale ends; prospects want to know when they can start.

Can the I-Date and the Contract Signing Date be the same date? Of course they can, if the prospect needs what the salesperson is selling that day. Movie tickets, last minute shopping, and impulsive buying are examples of instant sale/use. For the most part, when you are selling a big-ticket item to a company or corporation, and there are many different departments and processes that need to approve the sale, the dates will be different. From a ProActive Selling perspective, assume that for 90+ percent of sales in progress the I-Date and the contract signing dates are different.

The Implementation Date is the maybe killer. All qualified deals will have an I-Date. Salespeople usually know the I-Date in less than 50 percent of their current prospecting forecasts. There are three reasons for this.

1. Salespeople are focused on the selling process and do not know about a buy/sell process.
2. They don't think like a buyer and therefore focus on selling. They focus on the contract signing as the closing event for both parties.

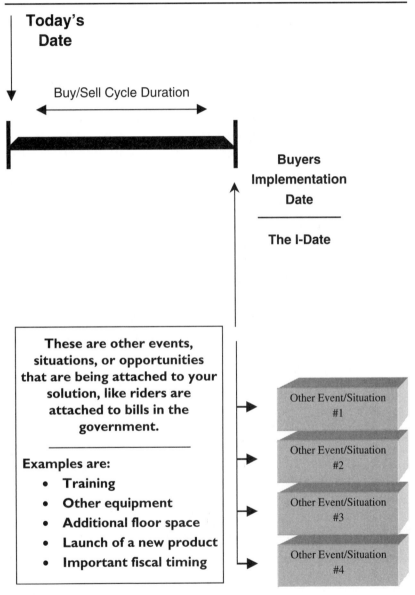

Figure 6-3. I-Plan bill of riders

3. They don't ask for the I-Date, assuming instead that it is ASAP.

In the worst-case scenario, the salesperson tries to juxtapose the buyer's Implementation Date to match the seller's contract sign date. Of course, this usually happens at the end of a year, the end of a quarter, or the end of a month.

"If you sign by the end of the month, we can give you a additional 10 percent off."

This is example of an out of control sale for two reasons. First, the salesperson is focusing on the contract sign date, not the Implementation Date. Second, because the salesperson cannot think like a buyer, he or she has to give a discount and buy the sale, a costly selling skill deficiency. What the ProActive salesperson would say in this case would be,

"Ms. Meyers, you have stated you would like this up and running by the fifteenth. Is there anything that would prevent us executing this agreement today and therefore giving you a 2-week cushion to make sure the implementation goes as smoothly as possible (risk)?"

The salesperson is thinking and selling in a buy/sell perspective.

Tool	**Question 3: Buy/Sell Steps—Buyers Buy Backwards**Tool

As discussed, knowing the buyer's I-Date will make or break a sales forecast. The I-Date is a very important tool, but it does have a limitation. The I-Date ensures a commitment by the prospect, where getting a commitment is a good thing to have. What the I-Date does not do is tell you how the prospect is going to buy. It does not give you the steps in the buy/sell process the buyer is going to go through or information on what direction the buyer is going to buy in—and buyers do buy in a direction. The Buyer Buy Backwards[Tool] gives you the buyer's buying direction.

The second question under Method is: What are the steps in the buy/sell process?

Finding out the steps in the process is important so that the salesperson and the prospect can agree on how to get from where they are today to where they want to be tomorrow. The problem is that most salespeople want the buyer to adapt to the salesperson's process and, at the end, close. Prospects are different, and at the end they make a decision; they do not close. Even worse, the reactive salesperson wants prospects to follow their sales cycle, which of course prospects do not want to do for two reasons: first, because it is not theirs, and second, it goes in the wrong direction—it goes forward instead of backward.

Sales people sell forward, but buyers buy backward.

SELLING FORWARD

"Ok, we are at the Educate step in this sale right now. What I want to do next is to schedule a meeting to complete the Educate process, and we should be done with that by the end of next week. Then I will give a demonstration so ownership transfers, which should complete the Validate step by the twenty-eighth. We can then complete the proposal by the following tenth, so they will make a decision by the end of next month. These are the steps I see the prospect taking for us to get to the close."

Many salespeople think this way. Selling forward is inherent in almost all sales strategies.

REACTIVE SALES STRATEGY DISCUSSIONS

Salespeople and their managers get together and discuss where a prospect is within a sales cycle, what the next steps are, so that the sales manager knows what to expect and where he or she can add value.

When does the salesperson think they are going to close this order, since it is on the sales forecast, and the sales manager wants to get this deal by the end of the quarter?

Do the salesperson's steps make sense? Has the salesperson presented these steps to the prospect, and has the prospect agreed? Does the sales manager have anything to add to the steps the salesperson has proposed so the sales cycle can be shortened or the competitive situation for this deal lessened?

Does this sound like a typical conversation you would have with your boss? The problem is that it goes in the wrong direction. Salespeople sell forward, but buyers buy backwards.

Salespeople are trained to think of a next step, then the next step, then the one after that, and so on, all the way until a close. This is good thinking. Proactive Selling's SBP is always pulling to a next step as well. However, next-step selling must be based on the prospect's buy cycle, not on the seller's cycle. Buyers buy backwards, not forwards.

Think about it. When was the last time you purchased anything of some importance? You bought it backwards.

- Last car: The lease on my car is running out on this date, so I need to do something about that soon.
- Last vacation: OK, we have to go on vacation the week of July 10. That is the only week all the kids are free. We need to finalize our plans soon.

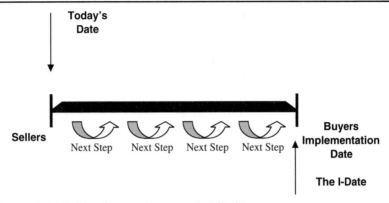

Figure 6-4. Selling forward—reactive thinking

- Last party: The surprise birthday party is going to be on the twentieth. We need to get the invitations out 3 weeks before, so we need to decide soon where it is going to be.

Last house, last set of golf clubs, last business suit, last computer, last . . . you get the point. Buyers start from a date, usually the Implementation Date, and they go backwards from there. Here is a typical conversation that goes on in a company, with individuals, the buyer, and anyone in the company who is involved in the decision, to make sure the Implementation Date can be met or needs adjustment.

"OK folks, we have to have this computer system up and running by July 1. That's 4 months away. What has to happen between then and now to make this happen?"
The group has a discussion on what has to happen. Purchasing has to be involved. The system specifications have to be finalized. The system has to be chosen among three vendors. Training has to be scheduled. There has to be time

for senior management approval. The list can go on and on.

The next conversation goes like this.

"Good, we now have a list of 20 things that have to happen

between now and July 1. Let's map these out to make sure

we can get all the things we need to do done, so we feel

good about making our July 1 date."

Buyers start from a date and go backwards. Once they have all the tasks and activities they need, they go backwards and adjust the schedule accordingly if they need to.

"I just can't make a decision this week because I will not

have to time to review the hardware implementation plan. I

can next week though, and it should not impact that July 1

date on this end."

This statement is a backwards statement. The buyer thought about what needed to get done, figured out how long she would need, and chose a date. Once the date was chosen, the buyer thought backwards to make sure there were no other conflicts, and that she had enough time to make the July 1 date (Implementation Date).

Now you have a problem. Salespeople make a sales call with their selling steps planned forward and present this process to the buyer. The prospect typically can understand what a salesperson is talking about, since all salespeople talk forward, and prospects are used to translating the forward discussion and then seeing if it fits into the backward process they have committed to. When prospects have to translate what you are saying into what they need to know, you have lost control of the sale.

To compound the problem, in the sales presentation the salesperson is proposing a next step. The buyer typically agrees with the salesperson's next step, the salesperson feels confident,

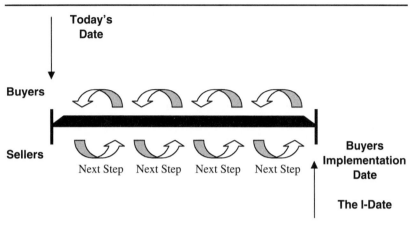

Figure 6-5. Buyers buy backwards.

asks for the next step, and the buyer agrees. The salesperson leaves feeling very good believing he or she is in control. They are in control, but of the wrong process. They are in control of the selling process, which of course the prospect has no commitment to, nor do they have any ownership of it. They have their own process.

Now, after the salesperson leaves, the buyer typically takes what the salesperson has proposed and tries to fit it into the buy process. If it comes close to matching, the buyer will feel good. If it does not, a salesperson may be eliminated from the process because the selling and buying processes did not match up, regardless of features and benefits. Worse yet, the prospect is always neutral, so who is in control now? It's not you, but your competition.

A ProActive salesperson must control the process and understand there is a buying process out there. BBB is a tool that states the salesperson must:

1. Understand that the buyer's process starts from the Implementation Date.
2. Identify the tasks and activities that the prospect has to accomplish.

3. Take the buyer's process, and go backwards from the I-Date. Then, once completed, they overlay the sales process with the buy process, and present this to the prospect for mutual agreement.

The prospect may then agree, may need to change some things, get some approvals, or do whatever he or she needs to do to formalize the process. If this sounds like a SalesMap, it is. The salesperson is now the one in control. He or she has taken the time to understand the prospect's buy process and even helped the prospect to identify some things that were missed, based on the selling organization's experience with other customers. Once the buy process is mapped out, the salesperson identifies the selling process, the things the selling organization needs to do, and the timeframe in which these tasks can be accomplished. (Too many sales are lost with, "Quick, we need a full demo of the system by next Monday. Who can we get, and how fast can we free up the schedule?") Armed with the buy process and the selling process, the ProActive salesperson can now overlay the two, look for discrepancies, fix these, and agree with the prospect on what needs to get done and by when.

The prospect feels good because the Implementation Date was used, not a selling or contract signing date. The prospect also feels good because the process has been identified from both sides. He or she believes all the bases have been covered, and their *risk level* has now decreased with this vendor, regardless of features and benefits. The salesperson is in control.

Buyers buy backwards, and salespeople sell forwards. It is the ProActive salesperson's job to:

- Identify the prospects' Implementation Date.
- Identify the tasks and activities the prospect has to accomplish.
- Identify what the selling organization needs to do.
- Get agreement from the prospect on all the activities.
- Eliminate any translation the prospect used to do when he or she was presented a sales cycle.

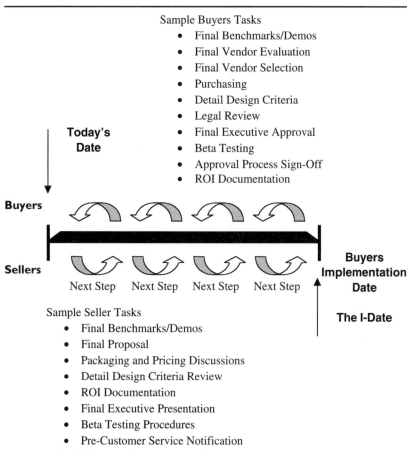

Figure 6-6. BBB with buyer and seller tasks that need to be accomplished

- Make the translation of the buying and selling processes a mutual process with the salesperson playing the conductor.

Control the process, win the deal. Since the ProActive sell process is based on the prospect's Implementation Date, the odds this deal will close, and close when the sales forecast says it will come in, are well above 50 percent, probably closer to 80 to 90 percent. Remember: BBB—Buyers Buy Backwards.

The GETS Chart: Buyers Buy Backwards Example

Very early in my selling career, the B.F. Goodrich Company was looking for some custom software development work to help its phone
system track and allocate costs to incoming and outgoing phone calls
for departmental budgeting reasons. There were three vendors bidding on this business, and we were one.

Vendors had to give a presentation on who they were and what
they could do for Goodrich. We flew in two senior consultants to help
make a presentation to Goodrich, and our meeting lasted more than 2
hours. We went back to the office and discussed what had happened.

Over the 2-hour meeting, Goodrich had discussed with us what
they had to do on their part to make their Implementation Date,
which was November 1. We told them what we would have to do to
make that date. Goodrich had laid out over 30 tasks that needed to be
accomplished, and we had close to the same number. Sixty activities
were laid out, and then it was time for the consultants to catch their
flight back home.

The next day, I was looking at all these activities, and I had no
idea what to do. I am a salesperson, not a project manager. Well, there
happened to be a project management consultant in my office named
Otto Bufe. Otto had walked by my cube and inquired on what I was
doing, and I explained. Otto then remarked, "Oh, that's a PERT (Program Evaluation and Review Technique) chart."

Not knowing what a PERT chart was, Otto proceeded to take
the 60+ "data points" and input them into a charting program. We
assigned time lengths to each activity and ordered them according to
which had to be accomplished first, second, and so on. We worked
backwards from the November 1 date, since this was the known
Goodrich I-Date. It was very rough, but Otto then ran the PERT program, and out came this color chart, complete with a critical path,
which we plotted on 24 × 36 chart paper. Goodrich's activities were
on the top of the chart, ours were on the bottom, and the timeline
was in the middle.

The following Monday, I took the chart down to Goodrich, and
we had a lively conversation around the chart itself. We adjusted activities, moved dates around, and reworked the chart. I went back to
the office, Otto ran another chart, and I sent it to our consultants.

They reworked their activities, Otto ran another chart, and a few days later, I went to Goodrich to get their buy in.

They were extremely pleased. They could see what they needed to do, and by when. It made their life simpler and lowered their risk of the unknown. They adjusted a few things, I went back to the office, and Otto ran a chart.

The evaluation and vendor selection took about 5 weeks. Twice a week, I would go down to Goodrich and discuss the chart. Internally at Goodrich, the project became known as GETS (Goodrich Electronic Tracking System). The chart became known as the GETS Chart.

I really do not know what my competitors were doing, or how much they were bidding for this project. I knew I had the GETS Chart. We had biweekly GETS Chart meetings. Goodrich used the GETS chart in its internal meetings with their management to get final approval of the project. Since we had our activities on the GETS chart, it basically became a nontransferable competitive advantage. Another vendor would have a very hard time plugging in its activities into our methodology. Goodrich wanted GETS. We had the Goodrich's Implementation Date, we had their process backwards, we had our process forwards, we had mutual buy in, and we had the GETS chart. We controlled the process and won the order.

There are countless numbers of GETS chart examples. ProActive Selling means that if you own the process, you own the deal. The GETS example is just one way of gaining and keeping control of the process.

Two of the three questions under Method have been answered.

1. What is the Implementation Date?
2. What are the steps in the buy/sell process, since buyers buy backward?

Question number 3 under Method is:

3. What is the Decision Criteria?

Tool   Question 4: The Decision Criteria™

What are the reasons buyers buy? There are hundreds of reasons prospects will end up buying from you, but in many cases, they end up buying for different reasons. It seems that many features/benefits are evaluated during the buy/sell process, and in the end the prospect buys for only two or three of these reasons. Decision Criteria is a tool that allows you to focus on the right two or three reasons and concentrate your efforts.

A prospect's buying decision comes down to five criteria. A decision to buy a good or service ends up focusing on:

1. Product or service features and benefits
2. Product quality
3. Professional support (also called ease of use)
4. Investment
5. Image

This is your buying pie, your PPPII, the five criteria on which a prospect will make a decision. In these five areas lie 99 percent or more of the buying reasons your prospect will use to make a decision to select you as a vendor or not.

Features and Benefits
This is the easy one. Salespeople can list pages and pages of items on these. Many of them have a competitive slant, rather than a prospect slant. Please remember the Law of Competitive Selling.

THE LAW OF COMPETITIVE SELLING

Buyers buy for their reasons, not how you stack up on a competitive issue. They do not care about your competitive issues. Demonstrate the Feature/Benefit/Value you provide and how it matches up against prospects' requirements and their competitive issues, not how you do things better/cheaper/faster than a competitor.

Figure 6-7. PPPII pie

Features/benefits and the value they provide are what are important in most sales presentations. Remember to stress the benefits, not just list hundreds of features and hope the prospect can sort them out and pick a few good ones. It's the reactive salesperson who wants to Spray and Pray, hoping that if he or she gets enough features of what they do out in front of the prospect, that prospect will be able to pick out the ones that are important to him or her. The reactive salesperson's motto is:

"Better to discuss too many features and overwhelm the

prospects than potentially leave something out."

This is reactive hit and miss selling. The Proactive salesperson does his or her homework, determines the needs of the prospect with the prospect, and then discusses features/benefits and value. ProActive Salespeople also de-emphasize features that are not important to the prospect, regardless of how important such features are to themselves. Too many car salespeople show customers the car engine, when some buyers tell the salesperson they do not care at all about the engine. For some fun, next time you are shopping for a car and see a reactive car salesperson, who just has to show you the engine, let him. When the salesperson opens the hood of the car, exclaim, "Yep, that's an engine alright. I wondered what was under that hood. By the way, it's a pretty engine too." This is a perfect response to a reactive salesperson.

The benefits are what count, but the features anchor the prospect, so make sure you state the feature and the benefit, as well as the value. You will find that, in most sales, it gets down to fewer than three features that are important. Work with the prospect to determine what they are, rather than be a reactive list generator.

Product Quality

Prospects look for quality when buying. How well is the product made, how will it stand up, how does it compare to similar products, and is the quality difference (towards or away) worth the price difference? These are some of the questions prospects are asking themselves. The prospect's interest in quality breaks down into five areas:

1. Good Enough Quality: This is quality adequate to meet the need. If a prospect is looking for a product that merely meets the need, quality is usually medium to low in terms of importance. Emotion has not yet entered into the evaluation, but in all likelihood, it will. If a prospect is interested only in "good enough quality," you can educate that prospect and move this priority higher within a prospective sale.

2. The Best Quality: If the prospect suggests that she needs the Best Quality, quality is obviously high on her list of reasons to buy. Emotional as well as logical business reasons are in play, and the prospect has chosen to allow emotions to dominate the value equation.

3. Comparative Quality: If the prospect is looking for only comparative quality, quality has not entered the decision process as an important factor, and probably will never be high up the priority list for a number of reasons. Usually, it is because one of the other PPPII factors is so dominant. It is very hard to move someone in this

area, since his or her other decision criteria are so high. You could spend a lot of time in this area, win the quality battle, and lose the war.

"They see everyone the same, even though they

admitted we may be better. They just do not rank

overall quality as high as I think they should."

This would be a comment from a salesperson who spent too much time pushing quality with a Comparative quality prospect and lost sight of the overall sale.

4. Time Quality: Time quality prospects play the short-term vs. long-term debate to the maximum.

"How long will I have it?"

"How long will I keep it?"

"How long will it be in use?"

"When will I not need it anymore?"

"When will I be replacing it?"

These are questions prospects ask when they view quality over time. Prospects who have a time definition to quality have to measure quality over time, and the astute salesperson addresses these quality/time issues.

5. Yesterday Quality: Here prospects assume quality based on history, image, reputation, personal use, or a host of other reasons. This assumed quality usually addresses the issue of risk. It is based on emotional logic and has no firm roots. A yesterday quality objection is one that is easily addressed if you take the high ground. You can introduce new information or discuss what has changed in the past year or so to overcome poor quality or reinforce good quality.

Professional Support/Ease of Use

Professional support/ease of use implies the service and support the prospect will be getting from the selling organization. This can take many forms:

- Training
- Installation
- Warranty
- Repair
- Engagement models
- 24/7 Support
- Hand holding
- Certification process
- Customer support
- Educational experience
- Extended warranty
- User interface
- Instruction manuals and documentation

The list can go on and on. Buyers want to feel they:

1. Will be taken care of (support for the risk element).
2. Can maximize their value (ease of use for the investment element).

If prospects emphasize professional support/ease of use, they are going to put the product/service to maximum use, or they are going into uncharted waters. If they need assistance while using it, there must be someone available to them to help them out.

These two issues speak volumes to Investment and Risk, two big points on the Value Star. Buyers want to get the most they can, but there is a balance between support (risk) and investment.

THE VALUE AXIOM

You can tell me what you want, and I will tell you how much it is, or you can tell me how much you want to spend, and I will tell you what you can buy. However, you cannot tell me what you want and how much you want to spend.

If you want a 25 percent discount at a retail clothing store, you cannot expect the same kind of service you would get at a high-quality retail store like Nordstrom where you pay full price. The manual and instructions for the $7,000 plasma screen TV will be very different than for the $99.00 9-inch portable TV. The instructions and support you get with the $29.99 software package are different from those of the $499.95 package. Buyers expect service and support when they pay a premium price. They expect a top-notch service organization. Satisfaction is directly related to their expectations, and because expectations of different prospects differ so widely, this is the area in which you can really make a competitive difference.

Buyers assume a lot, and they assume a similar level of professional support/ease of use from all vendors. All car dealers' services are the same. All retail, software, hardware, airlines, clothing, consulting, insurance, hotels, sporting goods, and electronic companies have the same service, right? Wrong. KPMG is not the same as Ernst and Young. Dell and Hewlett Packard are very dissimilar. Service, ease of use, and ease of doing business instill a unique kind of brand loyalty. It is the ProActive salesperson who knows that professional support/ease of use is a differentiator in the prospect's mind at all levels within the prospect's organization. Since you are the one who brings up the benefit and how what you offer supplies the benefit they are going to receive, it becomes a nontransferable competitive exclusive.

> *"You are asking for 24/7 help desk support. We offer that,*
>
> *and in this manner."*
>
> *"You want a company that can provide you up-to-the-minute*
>
> *information, and here's how we would do this for you."*
>
> *"Hello, this is the ABC Company, and you are talking to*
>
> *a live person. May I help you?"*

These are three examples of how you can use professional support/ease of use as an advantage. Identify the Features/Benefits/Value you offer that can fall into this category and act as competitive weapons in your sales process.

Investment

Investment is an area where you need to devote some quality time to preparation. With PPPII, Product Features is usually the category for which salespeople can generate a list that seems to go on and on. Product Quality and Professional Support are the ones that usually get the most discussion because they relate to the prospect's interest in your goods and services. Investment, however, seems to be the one for which most salespeople have the shortest bulleted list, because it is the one criterion that requires you to think like a buyer.

Prospects are not buying your product because it is neat, cool, the latest rage, or something they cannot live without. In this competitive market, there are so many alternatives prospects can choose from that it can get confusing to a buyer to decide what is the best investment of their resources. Buyers end up asking themselves two sets of questions. First, they ask themselves the *extremes* questions:

> *"What do need more of or less of?"*
>
> *"What do I need to increase or decrease?"*
>
> *"What do I need to amplify or diminish?"*
>
> *"What do I need extra of or a reduced amount of?"*
>
> *"Do I need it now or later?"*

Salespeople must always be able to answer *extremes* questions. By having your solution, product, or service, what will the prospect get more of or less of? All a prospect wants to do is increase something or decrease something.

The second set of questions buyers then ask themselves are the How Much questions. The rule about extremes questions is they must be quantifiable. If you do not get into specifics on what you are offering when addressing the extremes questions, your product or service will be viewed as a commodity. "It will increase your productivity" is a commodity statement, because it provides no quantitative value. All investment statements must be quantifiable. "It will increase your productivity by 25 percent over 2 years" is an acceptable Investment statement. Typical Investment comments are:

> *"Decrease time to market by 3 months."*
>
> *"Decrease your overhead by 17 percent annually."*
>
> *"Increase your market share by 2 points within 12 months."*
>
> *"Improve your margin on this product by 3 percent this fiscal year."*
>
> *"Increase production by 30,000 units/month."*

These are quantifiable monetary statements that Investment statements should speak to. Your product or service must address the Investment issue, and it must do so in a quantifiable way for it to be of any value to a vice president, let alone a CEO. Answer these two questions for every sale:

1. What extremes is the prospect trying to solve?
2. By how much?

It is about now that most salespeople say,

> *"Our product, however, does not make that big of an impact for our customers. We really are a small fish in a big pond. How can we make such a big difference?"*

The answer is obvious. Your prospect is willing to invest resources and spend money with you. So you have to make a difference to them.

Prospects are greedy; they want their money back, which is why they would give you any money in the first place. Your product does make a difference. It may not be the *thing* that gives the company a great return on a total investment it is making, but it is a very important piece of the whole. Find out the return the prospect is expecting from the whole, and then go from there. Do not be whittled down either. If a prospect is going to be saving $1,000,000/year with a specific project that your product is just a small piece of, your return is not only the value you add but also the value of the entire project. You may be worth a $10,000/year savings to the company, but with you in the equation, the larger $1,000,000/year has a degree of certainty to it. If someone else is in the picture other than you, the unknown factor increases, which means risk, and you know how buyers hate risk. The $1,000,000/year project has just become riskier, which Spaniards do not relate to, but Russians and Greeks hate.

Risk costs money. Do not let the prospect control the sales cycle and start dictating to you what you are worth. PPPII, especially Investment, is meant to differentiate you from being a seller or a financial partner with the buyer. Find out, quantitatively, what you are worth. Prospects know the numbers; all you have to do is ask the right questions.

Image

The final I in PPPII is for Image. Image or Brand is still very important. It is why people still spend more money on shirts that have a horse and polo player on them than they would for a shirt that did not have that logo. Image is the emotional play, and this is a very WIIFM area, so it therefore should be probed as such. Image can be obtained from many different areas:

- Company
  - Length in business
  - Size
  - Geographic location
- Product
  - Features
  - Benefits
  - Most used
  - Competitive advantage

- Customers
  - Certain industries
  - Certain market verticals
  - Showcase accounts
- Processes
  - ISO 9002
  - Industry certifications
  - Educational certifications
- Logo
  - Brand recognition
  - Partnership recognition
  - Trademarks and patents
- History
  - Length in business
  - Number of firsts
  - Number of bests
  - Reputation
  - Stability

Image has many different categories. What is important to understand is WIIFM. You must be the one who helps prospects with *their* image. Look at the preceding Image list and switch your focus to the prospects. How can you help them with their image? They want to improve their image, from a company, product, process, partnership, or many other perspectives. It is your job to make sure they see the value of doing business with you from their side, not yours. The fact you have been in business for 23 years is good, really good, but from the prospect's image perspective, they could care less. They want to be seen as doing business with only reputable firms, not any here-today, gone-tomorrow suppliers. The fact you have been in business that long may mean a lot to you, but to them it means you are helping them with their image. Image is not just what you think of yourself, or what the prospect thinks of you. It is about what the prospect thinks of themselves, and quite frankly, they are probably more interested in themselves than they are in you. Image needs to be looked at from both sides, not just what you have to offer.

Some rules to follow when you are using PPPII:

- The "So What" quiz—All PPPII questions must answer the "So What" quiz; it quantifies the PPPII questions.

  "Mr. Smith will be more productive because of the quality of our product and support."

  "So what?"

  "He will be able to cut costs."

  "So what?"

  "He said that cutting costs are his no. 1 priority."

  "So what?"

  "He will be able to report to his boss that he is cutting 22 percent of his overhead budget over the next 2 years, which is above his stated goal."

  "So what" questions are meant to quantify. In the above example, too many sales managers would allow the salesperson to stop at the first statement: since both the sales manager and the salesperson are very proud of their quality and support, it must be obvious to the prospect as well. This is thinking like a seller, and not like a buyer. "So what" questions make sure you really are thinking like a buyer. PPPII sets the stage. It puts you in the right ball field. "So what" questions make sure you remember that it is a buy/sell cycle, not the other way around. You want to probe as deep as you can into the answers given to you until you get the real answers from the prospect. Asking, "So what would that mean to you?" questions will help clarify the answers the prospect is giving you.

- Ask great questions. PPPII is a good tool. Most salespeople end up having 20 to 30 things under each letter. They do not want to leave anything to chance, and they want to be prepared. PPPII can have a lot of features associated with each letter. Great salespeople ask great questions, and PPPII is a great way for a ProActive salesperson to focus the sales call, and ask the right questions.

> *1—"Well Ms. Hamilton, what are you looking for?"*
>
> *2—"Well Ms. Hamilton, when it comes to the*
>
> *quality you require, or the amount of support that*
>
> *you will be needing, what is important to you?*

When you focus your questions on PPPII, you end up asking more pointed questions in an area to which the prospect wants to go, since PPPII is the prospect's decision criteria.

- Focus on one or two. Typically, a buyer focuses on one or two key criteria out of the five. Usually, it's the reasons other than product features. Sellers sell for product features. Buyers buy for the other four reasons.
- Competitive Issues. Having a list of PPPII things that you do and then having what they mean for the prospect will give you a competitive advantage. Your competition will not have an extensive list like PPPII. You will win because you have covered all areas and can easily access the few that are important to the prospect.
- Languages. Your PPPII should cover all three languages. You should have a PPPII in Spanish, Russian, and Greek. You never know who you are going to end up talking to.

The last question under Method, "What is the Decision Criteria?", is a very important question. It focuses you on the buyer's perspective rather than the seller's. It makes you ask great questions rather than blurt out answers, which ProActive salespeople would never do. It makes buyers quantify the investment they are making to you. It prepares you for sales calls because it will make you focus on what is really important to the prospect other than just features.

Motivation

The final three qualifying questions come under Motivation. What is really motivating the prospects to do something, and can you satisfy their need? The three questions are:

1. Is there a need?
2. Can you meet that need?
3. As a check, what are the top two benefits the prospect has specifically said she will get from implementing your solution?

These three questions will finalize the MMM qualification process.

Question 5: The Need

Is there a real need for your product or service, not an imaginary one, or one for which the salesperson can see the need but the prospect cannot. What has the prospect said her need is? A real need must address these issues:

- What is the reason for this need? (This is usually expressed in a towards or away direction.)
- How much attention is this getting? (This goes back to knowing the process.)
- What is the final outcome? What is going to change once a solution is put into place?
- How much is it worth? What is the financial or emotional gain?

When these questions are answered, you have a legitimate need.

Question 6: Can You Really Meet the Need?

Can you meet this need? To elaborate, you must have the knowledge of how, when, why, and what.

- How can you meet the need, and does the prospect agree?
- When does the prospect say he will implement a solution, and does this agree with the Implementation Date?
- Why would the prospect implement a solution?
- What is the overriding business case?
- What increases or decreases, and by how much?

Meeting the need is not just product fit. You must meet the business case need, the product fit need, and the process fit need. The sales world is full of unsigned sales deals because one or two of the above needs were unanswered. Can you meet *all* the needs is the right question here. Some examples include:

Business Case

- What is the ROI?
- What is the Risk?
- What Return on Assets are we getting?

Product Fit

- Does the product do what we want it to do?
- Is it the best of breed?
- Can it be leveraged into other areas?

Process Fit

- How does this fit with the way we are currently doing business?
- How much do we have to change the way we do things because of this?
- Can we make things more efficient?
- What other departments will this affect?
- Will communication change because of this change we are making?

All of the need questions have to be addressed for you to have a qualified prospect and a fit of your product/service to the prospect's needs.

| Tool | **Question 7: Top Two Client-Spoken Benefits** Tool |

The final qualification question is:

- What are the top two benefits the prospect has said he or she will receive by implementing your solution?

What are the top two reasons for which the prospect has said he or she would purchase your product/service? It should be not just any solution, or the overall solution, but your specific solution. What has the prospect said, specifically, in their words, about why they would make an investment with you? It must come from the prospect. Too many sales have been lost with,

"I haven't asked specifically, but I am sure they would

say . . ."

That doesn't count. What has the prospect said regarding why he or she would make a decision in your favor? At this point, salespeople usually ask the following questions:

"Well how do I know what they tell me is the real reason?"

"How do I know if they are telling me the truth?"

"How do I know what they tell me is what they really

mean?"

"Can they tell me one thing and really mean another?"

"How will I know when they really mean what they say?"

The following tool will help answer these questions.

Tool Three Levels of Why^{Tool}

The Three Levels of Why^{Tool} is a questioning technique that all good salespeople have mastered. It is a way for the salesperson to understand where the buyer is coming from.

There is a *real* reason why people make a decision, why you choose certain things. There is a real reason you wear the watch you wear, the car you drive, the shoes you own.

People do not like to talk about their real reasons, so they rationalize their decisions. Again, people do not like to discuss their rationalizations openly, so they develop rapport reasons to tell others why they made the choices they made.

Rapport reasons are the simple answers people have ready to answer rapport questions.

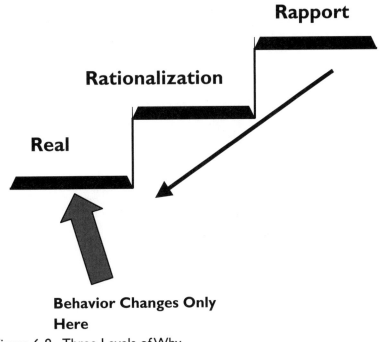

Behavior Changes Only Here

Figure 6-8. Three Levels of Why

"How are you feeling?"—"Fine."

"Why did you buy that camera?"—"I needed one."

"Where are you going on vacation this year?"—"Somewhere warm."

Rapport answers always sound good, but are at the top of the three levels of why, so there always is more to someone's decision process.

If these three levels of why are true going up, then the converse must be true, and you can change behavior only down at the third level of *why*. Rapport answers are typically what salespeople get when they ask questions in a sales environment. Good salespeople get down to the second level of why. ProActive salespeople know to go deeper and get to the third level of why. An example of Three Levels of Why:

"That's a really nice watch you are wearing. Why did you buy that watch?"

"I liked the color. I like a watch that has gold and silver."

(Rapport)

"I'm sure there were a lot of gold and silver watches. Why did you buy that watch?"

"I like the look. It is sporty, yet classic. I wanted a watch that you could wear every day, yet it would look good on special occasions." (Rationalization)

"I am sure there were many watches that were sporty yet classic. Why did you buy that watch?" (Real)

"You want to know why, I'll tell you exactly why. I just got a promotion at work, and I have always wanted this brand of watch. I bought the watch because I earned it."

This is an example of Three Levels of Why, and getting to the real reason. If you were a watch salesperson, you know why this person would buy a certain watch. You know the real reason. If you do not have the watch he or she is looking for, you now know the real reason why, and you can influence the buyer's behavior.

"I am sure that is a good watch, but people who just got the promotion they deserve usually look at this watch."

You now have a chance with this buyer because you know his or her real reasons for buying.

How do you know when you are at the third level of why? You just do. The nonverbal signs, the passion, the voice inflection . . . you know when you are there. How do you get there? You ask:

Why—"Why would you do that?"

What—"What would that mean to you?"

Flip—"So I think I hear you say this, is that correct?"

Three Levels of Why: The Beginning

I came up with the Three Levels of Why when I lost a deal. They say you learn more from your losses than your victories, and that's probably true.

I was selling computer-aided design and computer-aided manufacturing (CAD/CAM) systems many years ago. I was calling on a company in Akron, Ohio, a mold shop to be specific. They made plastic injection molds for the auto industry, and they were one of the largest in the area. It had been an 8-month sale cycle, and the deal was worth about $500,000. We were up against our number one competitor, who had the largest market share, was dominant in my territory, and had 10 times the sales volume we had.

I thought we had this deal done. We had done a good job, and I felt very secure in the probability we had for this sale. Our benchmark part, which both parties were required to do, looked so much better than theirs. I had posters and pictures of our CAD/CAM system in most of the engineers' cubes. This deal was ours for the taking.

Finally, the prospect company informed us they wanted to make a decision by the end of the week. They wanted one vendor to present at 10:00 A.M. on Friday, one to present at 1:00 P.M., and they would make a decision by 4:00 P.M. I positioned us to go at 1:00 P.M., and made sure we had a copy of an agenda that was approved by them. Basically, we had it wired for us to win the business.

Thursday afternoon, I called the chief engineer to make sure there were no questions. I drove down to Akron to be at their facility to make sure there were no competitors lurking about. At 5:30, the chief engineer told me he was going home. I walked him to his car to make sure everything was going in our favor.

In the parking lot on the way to his car, he turned to me and asked me a question. "Skip, do you and your system do XYZ as well as all the other things you have shown us?"

This was a great question. He was asking about a feature that we had, but it had no relevance to him, since he was a mold shop and would never need feature XYZ. It was a competitor's strength, but I knew I could convince him he would be wasting his money on such a feature.

"Dave, yes we have that feature, but quite frankly, you would never use it, and here is why . . ." I started in on my best sales pitch.

"You need to do business with a company that focuses its efforts on features that have relevance to you and what you need to do. Our company focuses on mold shops and has a great deal of understanding of the needs of companies like yours . . . blah, blah, blah." Dave agreed he would never need that XYZ feature. I handled that objection "perfectly."

The next day, our competitor gave his presentation at 10:00, we gave ours at 1:00, and at 4:00 we got a call saying they made a decision in favor of the competition.

I could not believe it. I was crushed. I knew I had the backing from everyone, so what happened? After a very mentally rough weekend, Monday I called Dave and asked for a meeting. We ended up going to lunch, and over that meal, this conversation took place.

"Dave, what happened?"

"Well when it came down to it, we liked your competitor's price. We saw all things as equal, and we decided that since your competitor lowered his price so that it was 10 percent lower than yours, we went with him." I thought about that for a while, but it didn't fit. It did not sound right.

"Dave, that doesn't sound right. Price never really entered into our conversations."

A few moments later, the conversation continued.

"Well, we really liked that one data entry feature they offered. We like the way an engineer enters data into their system better than yours."

I knew that was not completely true. The engineers who had participated in the demonstrations loved our data input method, so much so that they agreed to put pictures of our system in their cubes. This had to be a second level rationalization. I had nowhere to go, so I pressed on. It just did not make sense.

"Dave, I'm sure that had something to do with it, but I need to know. What was the real reason you chose the competition?"

After a long pause, Dave continued.

"You want to know why we went with your competitor, I'll tell you exactly why. I wanted your system more than the one we purchased. So did my engineers. Our chairman was a bit nervous spending $500,000 on a CAD/CAM system, though. That is a big expenditure for a company like ours. Your competitor realized that and offered all their other software, outside of what we were buying, to us for free. That made our decision swing toward them."

"But Dave, that doesn't make sense. You are a mold shop. You will never use all that other software, especially that XYZ feature. It does not relate at all to what you do."

"That's true, but our chairman figured out that we are going to be using the system only one shift per day. He has a lot of friends in the area who want to use a CAD/CAM system, but cannot afford it. So what we did was buy the system, load it with software that his friends can use, and then we are going to sell them time on the computer system. This way, he defrays his initial cost for the system and lowers his overall risk of the investment. We bought from them because they offered all their other software for free."

At that point, I said something like, "Well Dave, we can offer you that too!"

It was too late. In the parking lot the week before, when Dave asked me a question, I had done one of the stupidest things a salesperson can do. I answered his question. When asked a question at the first level of why, why did I have to answer it? What I should have done is used Three Levels of Why to find the real reason why he was asking me that question. I might have saved the sale.

Three Levels of Why is a tool to be used when you are asking prospects questions about why they are making a decision, especially why they would buy from you. Ask them what are the top two reasons they would make a decision in your favor, and then go to Three Levels of Why. How will you know when you get to the third level of why? You'll know . . . the emotion, the passion comes out. Emotion is at the third level of why, and you can argue that most if not all decisions are emotional first, then they are rationalized, and then rapport answers are created. A ProActive salesperson masters the Three Levels of Why to get to the real reason—the emotional reasons of why a prospect would make a decision.

MMM: The Seven Questions Reviewed

The questions that have been reviewed in this chapter are the master tools in the ProActive salesperson's toolbox. A qualified sales process is worth its weight in gold. There are many other qualification questions you can ask other than the seven listed here. It seems sometimes that you can never qualify a deal too much. The MMM qualification method is a way for a salesperson to get as much qualification information as he or she can in the beginning steps of the sale to make a logical business decision: "Should I continue on with this buy/sell process right now?" By knowing the answers to the MMM questions, and making sure those answers are positive toward your solution, the ProActive salesperson will have a better than 50 percent chance of winning the sale. Control the process, and you will control the sale. Control the process, qualify, and you will win more sales than ever before.

Money
1. What is the process?
   a. To obtain funds?
   b. To obtain a decision?

Method
2. What is the Implementation Date?
3. What are the steps in the buy/sell process?
4. What is the Decision Criteria—PPPII?

Motivation
5. Is there a need?
6. Can I meet that need?
7. Top two client spoken benefits—Three Levels of Why

Chapter 7

Validate

You are making progress on controlling the process. You started the process with generating initial interest. You did your homework. You figured out when to call, who to call on, and where to spend your time. You have learned languages appropriate to three corporate levels, so you can speak the right language to the right person all the time. Then armed with your 30-second speech, you made the first sales call. You got the prospect's attention and interest, then you Summarized, Bridged, and Pulled (SBP) to the Education phase. You did a good job of sales education and developed a SalesMap. During the Initial Interest and Education stages, you were qualifying to MMM and the seven questions, and you now feel you have a better than 50 percent chance of winning this deal. You SBP, and now you are in the Validation stage.

Buyers now understand what you are offering, and you understand what the prospect needs. Both the prospect and the salesperson want to take a next step. The problem is they usually are two different steps, and if the salesperson is not careful, he or she can lose control of this sale, and potentially lose this deal.

The salesperson wants to start closing this sale. He wants to "put some numbers together" or "sit down and work something out" or "get together and see what makes sense." A salesperson figures,

> *"I now know what they need, they know what we offer.*
>
> *Everything looks good, so let's get this done."*

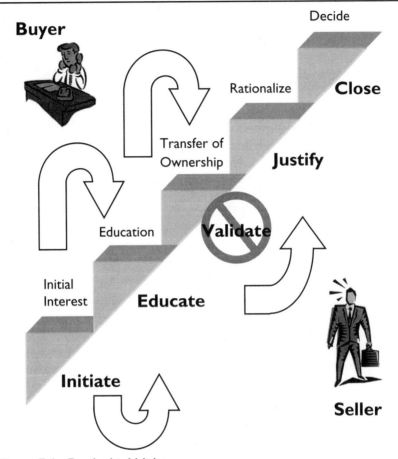

Figure 7-1. Don't skip Validate.

Now is the time to slow down. The prospect is not at that stage yet. He or she needs to understand what this solution is going to do for him or her, exactly how it is going to work, and exactly what the final benefits are going to be, both to the company and to the prospect personally. The prospect needs transfer of ownership; the seller needs to close this deal: Major accident waiting to happen.

The ProActive Initiation of Transfer of Ownership

At this point in the buy/sell process the prospect wants to understand what the solution is going to look like.

> *"What is this going to specifically do, and how will the re-*
>
> *sults of what I am buying come to pass?"*
>
> *"What will my world be like if the solution you are offering*
>
> *me actually comes into being?"*
>
> *"What will be different?"*
>
> *"What will change?"*
>
> *"Will it really work as claimed?"*

This is what prospects are thinking. It is the next step in their process. They do not want what the salesperson is offering right now: a proposal or a contract. They really don't. They would agree to one now only because:

- You as a reactive salesperson are forcing one on them.
- They do not fully understand what you are selling, so they are hoping your proposal will shed some light on their lack of education, which is why they are asking for one. (You are now in limbo. The prospect is still looking to be educated, and you are trying to validate.)
- They need to know their options so they can envision the full solution. (They are in the Validation stage, and you are in the Justify stage.)
- They are in control of the sale and you are just doing what you are told to do.

None of these options seems to be a good choice, but salespeople consistently find themselves in these dilemmas. Why? It's because salespeople do not fully understand the validation step. The prospect needs to take ownership. You do the same when you buy. Here are some examples.

- Shoes: Most people would never buy a pair of shoes without trying them on. "Well, I have to see if they fit." Why do stores spend so much money on those floor mirrors? People have to see what they look like in these shoes, as well as what other people will see when they look at them. Then they also have a discussion with the salesperson on how these shoes would look with other clothes. The buyer has started the process of taking ownership of the shoes.
- Software: Did you ever wonder why software companies spend so much money on packaging? They show screen shots of the actual product, especially games. They are trying to get the user to experience the actual software. They are trying to create a visual transfer of ownership.
- Cars: The test drive has become a standard.
- Televisions: Try to buy a TV without trying out the remote control. Retail stores sell more TVs when they attach the remote control to the TV, which is why you see so many remote controls in all the TV stores.
- Computers: This is a good one. Computer stores display all the latest computers, and you have to try it out before you buy it. You see a computer monitor, mouse, keyboard, and preloaded software—all the same equipment you already have. The computers that are lined up at the store are basically all the same, but you still have to try out the one you want to buy; see if you can buy a computer without going up to one and trying it out.

    Apple has you buying a computer for the color, design, and image, which have nothing to do with computer functionality. What are you actually doing when you are trying out a computer? You are not learning anything. You are transferring ownership.

Prospects are not educating themselves at this point in the buy/sell process. They are validating their educational experience. This is what prospects need to do at this point, and what salespeople need to learn about and control. The preceding examples are easy ones, but you can give an example of any product and service, and it would still hold true.

It's Validation, Not Education!

In this phase of the buy/sell cycle, prospects want to transfer ownership of the proposed solution to their needs. They need to digest fully the entire picture. The brain is filtering information and creating a picture so the prospect understands what is being offered. He or she is not learning anything new at this time; they learned what they needed to learn in the Educate phase of the process. Now is the time for prospects to validate their educational experience, to prove to themselves that the shoes fit and look just right, the TV does respond to the remote, and the display samples of the software product do indeed look like they're something he can handle and use effectively.

Think about the car test drive. You educated yourself on the car you wanted. You might have spent months learning about this vehicle, or just 10 minutes. Whatever the time frame you used, you did educate yourself on the car. Then you needed to validate your educational experience, so you took the car for a test drive. During that drive, you did not educate yourself. You checked whether the car handled and felt like you expect it to, whether it lived up to your educational experience based on quality, feel, and overall satisfaction. You were validating your educational experience.

Now some of you are saying,

"Wait, I really do test drive the car to learn more about the performance or about the overall feel of the car. It is important in my decision, and I am learning, not validating anything."

VALIDATION ≠ EDUCATION

Figure 7-2. Validation Is Not Education

You are right. A demonstration of a product or service can validate an educational experience. It can also educate. Do not confuse the issues.

- *The act of a demonstration can be for educational or for validation purposes.* It is all in how you, as a salesperson, set it up. The demonstration of a software product can be used to educate the prospect on the features of the system. The demonstration of a software product can be used to validate the use a prospect has in mind for the system. In the first case, the prospect is learning. In the second, the prospect is validating and taking ownership of something he or she has already learned.
- *Prospects need to Educate and Validate in two separate steps.* Salespeople believe they can Educate and Validate in one step. This just isn't true, and if you try to do it, it will lead to miscommunication between the buyer and the seller.
  - "We had a great demo. We showed them what we wanted them to see, and we performed flawlessly." This is Education, not Validation.
  - "We had a great demo. We showed them what they asked to see and then went into the conference room and discussed at length how they are going to use it." This is Validation, after an Educate step. Two different steps are taking place in the same meeting, which is fine.
  - "I was telling them exactly what we do. I know they got it. They were asking great questions about what we do and what our plans are for the future. After lunch, they diagrammed out how they are going to use our solution." This is a good Validate after an Educate step. It is an example of Transfer of Ownership.

The act of demonstrating a product or service, from a pair of shoes to an automobile to a multimillion dollar service implementation, can be in the Education phase or the Validation phase. You need to make sure you do both and do them in two different steps, even if it is in the same meeting.

The brain has a hard time educating and validating at the same time. When it is in education mode, it is learning. It is receptive, and new information is being acquired. When it is in validation mode, it is doing something very different. It is rationalizing to itself what it has learned. It is asking itself, "How am I going to use this?" "Is this the right thing for me?" "Can this be used for what I want to use it for?"

In the third preceding example, the salesperson's drawing out what they do was education. If the prospects were asking questions about the product/service being offered, that was education too. If the prospects were asking questions about how they would be using the product/service, or when it would be delivered, then transfer of ownership is starting. When the prospect starts to diagram out specifically how it is going to fit into their current process, then transfer of ownership is really beginning to take hold.

Prospects are now satisfied that they have learned something and understand what it will do for them, usually both for themselves and their company. This is the process of validation or transfer of ownership, and if you think it all happens at the same time, you are in the same boat as many reactive salespeople. ProActive salespeople know that they must educate and validate at different times. It could happen on one sales call, in which after the educational part of the presentation, the salesperson asks the prospect, "Now that we have explained what we do, and how you would use it, how do you see what we have been talking about benefiting you and your company?" This break in thinking for the prospect, from education to figuring out WIIFM, is the difference between Educate and Validate, and the ProActive salesperson would *never* go from Educate to Justify without transfer of ownership, or the Validate step. The temptation to skip a step is very high. The prospect may be anxious for a proposal. The competitive bids may be due in the next day. The prospect has told you this is the next step, and you really believe him. These are all valid reasons, but if you make the jump from Educate to Justify, you will lose control of the sale, be on the path headed to maybeland, and may never figure out why you are not making your quota.

Let the Buyer Drive: ProActively Inducing the Transfer of Ownership

So now that you know the difference between education and validation, the question is, How do you get prospects to validate your information so it makes sense to them and, once that happens, continue on the buy/sell process in your favor? Maybe that's not what you were thinking exactly, but it's close.

You have two choices. Prospects can come up with the validation by themselves, or you can assist them. You can have the prospect do all the work and hope they come up with a solution that is in your favor, or you can ProActively induce the transfer of ownership. The goal, obviously, is to learn how to keep control of this buy/sell cycle, and ProActively induce transfer of ownership. ProActive salespeople know they must sell for themselves, because to give control to the prospect right now will lead you towards maybeland. So how do you keep control of the sale, have the prospect take ownership of your solution, and learn how to induce transfer of ownership ProActively? Believe it or not, that's the easy part, because this one is all up to you. It is all in how you prepare for it.

How you prepare for a validation process will determine how successfully the prospect takes ownership. The prospect has two choices, to take ownership or not. You must assume he or she wants a solution to his or her needs, so assume the prospect is going to take ownership to someone's solution. The two choices the prospect has are:

1. Are they going to be in control of taking ownership? or
2. Are they going to let you have control?

Most prospects want control, so to take control away from them, and, in doing so, have them trust you with that control is the key issue. You will now learn how to take or keep control during this key part of the sale and ProActively induce transfer of ownership.

Many tools are available to a salesperson to induce the transfer of ownership:

- Client visits
- Brochures
- Testimonials
- Home office visits
- Trials
- Test drives
- Pilot programs
- Money back guarantees
- Samples
- Custom demonstrations

The list can go on and on. Salespeople can use all the tools they currently have at their disposal to help the prospect transfer ownership. Yes, these are the same tools a salesperson uses to educate the prospect. But the difference between Educate and Validate, from a selling perspective, is in preparation and how it is set up. How you set up the transfer of ownership step the prospect wants to go through is what makes the difference.

The key to transfer ownership ProActively is to manage expectations. One needs to get prospects to commit to making a decision before the transfer of ownership takes place. If they see what they want to see, if their expectations (which have already been stated up front) are met, they will commit to a buy. The best transfer of ownership demonstrations happen before the transfer of ownership takes place. The salesperson asks questions and has a conversation with the prospect about:

- The education they have already had
- What it means to them
- What they would do with the solution if they had it now

An example:

> *"Well Mr. Smith, we have had a good series of meetings so far. This morning, we had a demonstration to educate you and your team on the range and depth of our software. Any questions so far?"*
>
> *"No, not really. I think we have a good understanding of what you can do. I think we are ready for you to send us a proposal, complete with numbers, so we can get a good handle on the costs and implementation schedule."*
>
> *"Great."*

This sounds like a good meeting so far. The salesperson has done his homework and is in a good position. He has used a demonstration of the software system to educate the prospect on what the system can really do. The salesperson now has two choices. He can jump to a proposal just like the prospect has suggested, or he can ProActively induce transfer of ownership.

Choice 1

> *"That sounds like a great idea. Why don't we put a proposal together and I will personally drop it off to you next Friday."*
>
> *"Perfect. We are anxious to get this project going."*

Choice 2

> *"That sounds like a great idea, Mr. Smith. We want to make sure our proposal meets your actual requirements. Before we deliver a proposal, we need to discuss the implementation. We have scheduled some time this afternoon to*

discuss the implementation schedule for this project. To

begin, could you describe to us, once a system like this is

implemented, what your expectations would be? What

would be happening in your organization and in others

that would be affected by a new system such as this?"

Clearly, these are two different approaches. In Choice 1, the client has taken control, the salesperson is following what the client wants, and the salesperson has left the transfer of ownership up to the client. In Choice 2, the salesperson has control and knows that transfer of ownership has yet to be achieved. The salesperson wants to move the prospect to the Validate phase of the buy/sell cycle and does so by asking the prospect to describe what his operation would be like if he had the software up and running right now. The salesperson just used a tool called the Time Demo to begin the transfer of ownership.

Tool   **The Time Demo**Tool

For the most part, the brain has no natural way of telling actual time. The brain is given frames of reference with which to tell time: seconds, minutes, hours, days, weeks, months, years, and so on. With these constraints or rules, you can organize your thoughts, appointments, and your time.

The mind, however, can travel in time. It can go back and remember as well as go forward and imagine. This time travel capability of the mind is a very powerful tool to be used in transfer of ownership.

Here is how a Time Demo works. It is a three-step process. You discuss what today's reality is. You then discuss what tomorrow's reality is. Then you discuss what the prospect would be doing if tomorrow's reality actually happens. These end up being future benefits, which will happen only if the prospect implements your solution.

What do you think these future benefits are? They are the hopes and dreams of the prospect.

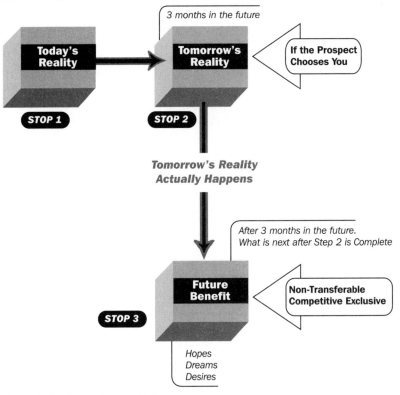

Figure 7-3. Time Demo^{Tool}.

"Well, if I had this up and running, and everything was working well, I would be able to then take on my next project, which I have been waiting for months to tackle."

"So if I had this TV in my living room right now, I wouldn't have to fight my kids over what I want to watch. I would be able to go to the other room and watch what I wanted to watch for a change."

"If this project was implemented, the return on this investment would fuel our new product development team and

give them about 3 months head start on that new project. I

can tell you my president would be really happy about that."

These future benefits the prospect is dreaming about are now mentally a part of your proposal, since you were the one who had this discussion with the prospect. They will anchor their future benefits to your solution, and become a nontransferable competitive benefit for you. Some additional rules about Time Demos are:

- The prospect is going to have this future benefits conversation with someone, so it might as well be you. Prospects need to look out into the future and be comfortable with their fear of the unknown before they will move forward. You need to discuss with them what their life is going to be like once the solution is in place. Moving from Step 2 to Step 3 is critical in a Time Demo. They are not going to ask you to implement what you are selling. They need to do that and "see" the future.
- They may try to make the benefits generic, more company oriented than personal. For Time Demos to work, they must be personal as well as company oriented in nature. What is in it for them as a company *and* as an individual must be answered.
- If they try to keep their future benefits a secret, you are probably dealing with the wrong person or are in a bad competitive position. Prospects who have decision authority, those who have the biggest stake in the game, are the ones who want to share and usually elicit help, especially with someone with whom they are going to do business.
- Time discussions should be visual because 70 percent of the world wants to "see" the benefits. Make sure you create the mental picture in the prospect's mind. Use charts, graphs, overheads, wipe boards, and flipcharts. Use these visual tools to make it interactive as well as visual.
- Make sure the Time Demo discussions are in the right language, since the benefits to each level in the prospect's organization are different.

- Keep the prospect involved. During the Time Demo, you should be acting like a conductor, not first chair violin in the orchestra. Let the prospects assimilate the benefits to them in the future; do not merely tell them and hope they "get it."

What's Your Dressing Room?

A friend tells a story that solidifies the concept of transfer of ownership and the need for a prospect to go through a Validation phase.

He was a services salesperson dealing with Fortune 100 customers. His average deal size was $500,000, and he carried a 4.5 million dollar quota. He knew selling and knew all about completing the transfer of ownership.

He was talking to his wife Nancy about selling and transfer of ownership in a buy/sell process. Nancy made a statement that transfer of ownership selling is the difference between Nordstrom and Macy's. She had sold for Nordstrom for 11 years, and for many of those years she was a Pacesetter, which is the top sales ranking a Nordstrom salesperson can achieve annually.

He discounted her expertise. "Retail selling is not real selling. There is no real prospecting, sales cycle, or qualification skills in retail sales. Business-to-business selling, where the solution is mutually agreed to, and the value runs into the tens and hundreds of thousands of dollars, is very different," he claimed.

She was adamant in her position. "I will take you down to Nordstrom and show you that we solution sell at Nordstrom, and transfer of ownership is our number one goal. You see, my job at Nordstrom, and how I became a Pacesetter, was not to sell people clothes. My job was to get the customer in a position where I had a better than 50 percent chance of winning. If I could do that, I had a good chance of closing the sale."

"How did you get the customer in a better than 50 percent probability of closure situation?"

"Come on down to Nordstrom and see for yourself."

So they went and stopped in where she used to work, in a women's sportswear clothing area called Point of View. They stayed on the outside perimeter and observed. Within a few minutes, they observed a husband and wife shopping. The wife had a blouse and two pairs of pants, and was shopping for a few more items. Her husband, who was shopping with her, looked like a typical husband who is shopping with his wife; he was fidgety, constantly looking at his watch, and clearly not in a place where he wanted to spend a lot of time.

A Nordstrom salesperson approached the couple, and did what my friend claims is one of the dumbest things he has ever seen in sales.

She walked right up to the wife and did not say, "Can I help you?" like most retail store clerks reactively do. She walked up to her and said, "May I reserve a dressing room for you?" To my amazement, the wife gave the salesperson the clothes she had on her arm, and then the salesperson proceeded to go to the back of the department where the dressing rooms were and hung up the clothes in a dressing room."

This had to be a selling faux pas, since the buyer at that time did not have any ownership. She did not have the clothes in her possession, there was really nothing keeping her in the store, and she really was free to leave. I looked at my wife to tell her that once again, retail selling is very different than real selling, when all of a sudden, the husband realized his wife did not have the clothes she had picked out and made his move. "Honey, I'm sorry you really couldn't find what you were looking for, but we really have to go soon. It's getting late." She quickly turned to her husband and said, "We can't go . . . they've reserved a dressing room for me." She then marched past her husband to the back of the store and went into the dressing room area to find where her salesperson had put her clothes.

A few minutes later, she appeared from the dressing room with one of the outfits on. She asked her husband what he thought. Guess what the husband had to say? "You look good in that one." He probably knew that if he said "It's just not you," or "You can do better," that's exactly what she would do, to continue to shop until she found something else. So the husband had two choices, say it looks good and let her decide if she wanted to buy it, or to say he didn't like it and she would continue to shop.

He was really enlightened when his wife turned to him and said, "Do you think the Nordstrom salesperson doesn't know this is what exactly is going to happen? For me, a salesperson's job at Nordstrom is not to sell clothes. Her job is to sell dressing rooms. She knows if she gets the customer to try the clothes on, she has a better than 50 percent chance of closing the sale. Our transfer of ownership vehicles are the dressing rooms."

She continued. "You see, that's the difference between Nordstrom and Macy's. At Nordstrom, we sell dressing rooms. Our dressing rooms are lively and very well appointed, where you do not mind spending shopping time. With so many mirrors and elevated dressing platforms that make you look slimmer, you just have to look good. Also, no one ever thinks to ask for a discount on a dressing room. At Macy's, I wonder sometimes if they even have dressing rooms. The ones they have are not as well laid out or as nice as the ones at Nordstrom. Nordstrom makes the dressing room a part of the sale, whereas Macy's thinks it is where you go to try on clothes. They let buyers go there by themselves, so the salesperson is not really in control of the sale. Since Macy's sells clothes, to get a 10 to 30 percent discount at Macy's is much easier than at Nordstrom. I ask for discounts at Macy's all the time, and I usually get one. At Nordstrom, it is almost impossible to get one."

Nordstrom sells dressing rooms and usually always sells at list price, and the salesperson works the dressing room as a transfer of ownership device. Macy's sells clothes, usually discounts, and the salesperson is there to close the sale, but does not work the process. Transfer of ownership does indeed happen even at the retail sale level. It is all in the setup.

How do you induce transfer of ownership ProActively? How do you make sure you allow the prospect to take ownership and help you in the sales process? What tools could you use right now as transfer of ownership tools rather than just educational tools? What is your dressing room?

A final note on the Validate phase: During the process of Transfer of Ownership, it is possible to have a bad Transfer of Ownership experience. During this time, the prospect does learn something new or thinks of something that now becomes important to the entire process. When this happens, the options you have are:

- Further questioning: Use the Three Levels of Why to find out the real objection and overcome it.
- More detail: What is the real reason something has become important, and can it be addressed by the current solution? Does it have a logical or emotional basis? Usually it is emotional, so probe for fears.
- Go back to the Educate process. You have missed something, and the prospect is going no farther until this issue is settled.

Validate is the step in the buy/sell process that most salespeople forget. Salespeople are so interested in getting to the next step that it is easy to run right over the prospect's need to complete transfer of ownership. A salesperson hears the prospect say, "I get it," and actually believes he or she does, and goes for the close. The ProActive salesperson knows the difference between, "I get it" and "I got it." "I get it" means the prospect understands and his or her education is complete. The prospect got what you have been describing about your product/service. "I got it" means he or she not only understands what you are selling, but also how he or she is going to use your solution to improve what he or she is doing and how he or she is going to make money at it. This is a big difference—the ProActive difference.

If Validate is the step most people skip, Justify is the step where more salespeople lose control of the sale than in any other step in the process. It is now time to leave Validate and go to Justify.

Chapter 8

Justify

Now the prospect has taken a big step. They understand what you are offering, and they have taken ownership of it. The prospect is moving along a path to make a decision. They make a stop before they are willing to commit, however, at Justify.

The Justify part of the process is where the prospect needs to rationalize the decision they are going to be making. It's when you go out and look at the car once more before you by it. You drive by the house you are ready to make an offer on one last time to be sure you haven't overlooked anything. The prospect asks for one more demonstration, has one last set of questions, or needs to have a top level overview before he or she can continue.

Many things happen in the Justify phase. The prospect is having second thoughts, or is trying to rationalize the purchase, or is putting a final evaluation on the risks and the ROI analysis. The prospect is in the home stretch, and the one thing that will keep you on the path of getting this sale is to maintain control of the process.

There are three tools in this chapter that will help you to get the prospect to make a decision, which salespeople call the close. The goal for the ProActive salesperson in the Justify phase is to overcome any last minute objections, work with the prospect to ensure that you are in the best competitive position possible, and SBP the sale to the last phase of the buy/sell process. The ProActive tools for Justify are:

- Institutional and Individual Reasons^{Tool}
- Implementation Plan^{Tool}
- Drop, Push, Pull^{Tool}

Tool   Institutional and Individual Reasons^{Tool}

Prospects will always have two sets of reasons for their decision in a sale. There are the Institutional reasons and the Individual reasons. The ProActive salesperson makes sure they have both of these reasons identified and addressed for every sale.

The Institutional reason is one that has its focus on the company or the institution. Typical Institutional reasons prospects give are:

- Return on investment
- Increase competitiveness
- Return on assets
- Decrease overhead
- Increase revenue
- Less risk to the business
- Strategic advantage
- Product diversification

These reasons center around advantages the company will receive if the solution you are offering is implemented.

Individual reasons are ones that benefit the prospect or members of the prospect's team personally. There is an advantage in the solution for them. Individual wins focus on WIIFM. Individual reasons have a personal slant and are usually very emotionally based. They are very dominant in the decision process.

- It will get the boss off my back.
- It will put me in line for a promotion.
- It is tied to an executive compensation program.
- It will free up time for me to do other things.
- It will allow me to do more of what I really want to do.
- I'll be able to implement something I have always been interested in.
- It will give me more power in the company.
- It will help me and my team to do something that helps a lot of other people.

Which reason, Individual or Institutional, do you think shows up in company ROI documents? Which one do you think is the real reason why people make decisions? The important thing is that a ProActive salesperson knows both for every deal. Just having one without the other opens you up to competition. It gives them an opening to exploit. A salesperson usually knows one or the other, and is usually happy with it.

> *"The reason they want to buy from us is that it will lower*
>
> *their cost."*
>
> *"Jim wants this solution. He has been looking forward to*
>
> *this project for months. It will finally give him the credibil-*
>
> *ity he has been looking for."*
>
> *"The company needs this for their expansion."*

It is easy to pick out the Individual and the Institutional reasons. Make sure you have them both, and do not get lulled into thinking that one is sufficient. You need Institutional reasons to help the prospect develop an ROI document and to have discussions with upper-level managers (those Russian and Greeks again). You need to have Individual reasons because most if not all decisions are emotional, as has been demonstrated with Three Levels of Why.

Tool The Implementation Plan^{Tool}

It is now during the Justify phase that the prospect may start to get a bit nervous. Is this expenditure the right one? Do we need to look at other vendors? Is this really the right time to make an investment like this? The pressure for a prospect to stray from a SalesMap can get very strong. You can keep the prospect in line and on track with an Implementation Plan.

The Implementation Date was discussed in Chapter 6. You know that a prospect has an Implementation Date, and you know that Buyers Buy Backwards (BBB). With this information,

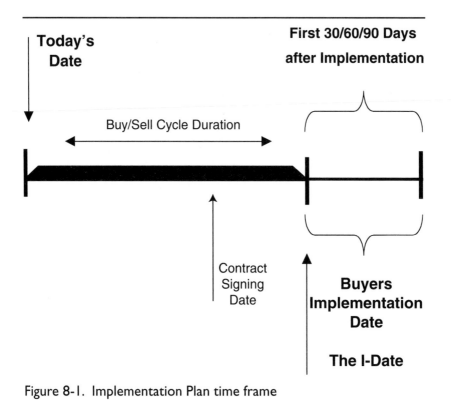

Today's Date

First 30/60/90 Days after Implementation

Buy/Sell Cycle Duration

Contract Signing Date

Buyers Implementation Date

The I-Date

Figure 8-1. Implementation Plan time frame

you developed a SalesMap that you have been working on since Educate. You and the prospect are now in the Justify phase of the buy/sell process, you are getting close to decision time, and closing in on the time when prospects need to sign an order so they can meet their Implementation Date. To make sure you are in control and can validate your control of the process within all levels in the organization, you need to develop an Implementation Plan.

Most selling organizations are focused on selling a product or service, as well as making sure that the prospect, who once he or she purchases is no longer a prospect but is a buyer and a customer, fully utilizes the product or services that are being sold. To do that, most selling organizations agree that the first 30 to 90 days after the buyer's Implementation Date are very critical. This first 30 to 90 days or so is the time when the buyer

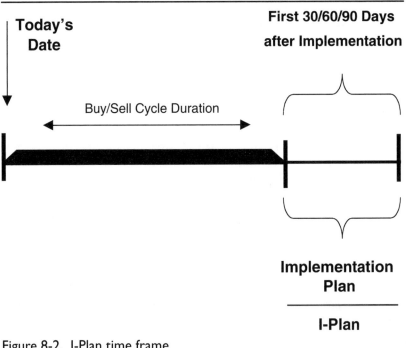

Figure 8-2. I-Plan time frame

starts using the solution he has purchased and begins a customer relationship with your company.

If customers work hard to use the goods/service they have purchased from you in the first 30 to 90 days after implementation, it goes a long way in determining how satisfied the buying and selling organizations are going to be. The customers who do a great job of planning and spending time in the first 30 to 90 days, really stretching the solution they have purchased, end up being the most satisfied customers. It is very important, then, that prospects have a plan of action for those first 30 to 90 days after they take delivery. You now need to develop an Implementation Plan to help the buyer through those first 30 to 90 days. You need to develop it not only for the sake of a satisfied customer, but also for you to win the sale. What is an Implementation Plan, or I-Plan?

The I-Plan is a one-page document, typically written in value-based language (Russian), to help the upper management of the buying organization determine whether it is effectively using its resources as well as using you, the selling organization, to its maximum return on the investment. The I-Plan outlines the top five or so areas that management of the buying organization should focus on internally to make sure its implementation team is doing its job effectively. You have gathered this information by working with individuals in the prospect's organization and by referencing successful implementations of your product or service with previous customers. You are giving the management of the buying organization a list of items that they need to oversee to ensure their people are going to do their job well. Senior management is always looking for a map of what measurable objectives it should focus on to maintain top performance in its organization, and you have taken some of the guesswork (and therefore some of the risk) out of it.

In addition, your I-Plan includes the five or so objectives that the customer management team should hold you, the vendor, to. Your prospect's management is spending a lot of resources on you and your organization. They want a return on this investment, and they want the return to have low risk and yield a maximized amount of money in the shortest amount of time. By giving the buying management a list of objectives it needs to hold you to, you are helping them to accomplish these goals.

Many organizations have implementation plans that are assembled after the purchase has been made. It is a customer service document that companies work on with their customers to implement the solution at the user level. How does an I-Plan differ from other user-centric implementation plans?

- An I-Plan is a selling document. It is used during the sales process, not after. It should be used to assess your position in the sale and help determine your competitive position and your next step.
- An I-Plan is written in Russian. You use it to get back in to see the vice president. You have been working with all languages, and you need to make sure the top executive in the process is on board. Even if you are being blocked by a manager (Spaniard), you can use an I-Plan to get

Developed exclusively for: _____

Project _____

Implementation Date _____/_____/_____

Key Items that the ABC Company should monitor internally and watch during the first 30–90 days after implementation:

	Complete?	Date
1. _____	☐	_____/_____/_____
2. _____	☐	_____/_____/_____
3. _____	☐	_____/_____/_____
4. _____	☐	_____/_____/_____
5. _____	☐	_____/_____/_____

Key Items that the ABC Company should monitor internally and watch during the first 30–90 days after implementation:

	Complete?	Date
1. _____	☐	_____/_____/_____
2. _____	☐	_____/_____/_____
3. _____	☐	_____/_____/_____
4. _____	☐	_____/_____/_____
5. _____	☐	_____/_____/_____

This document should be reviewed at least weekly the first 30 days, then bi-weekly until the 90-day mark. A business review should be held at the 90-day mark to assess and take additional action if required.

Figure 8-3. Executive implementation plan worksheet

back up to the decision maker, since it is written in value-based language, and for 15 to 20 minutes of their time, you are going to maximize their investment and lower their risk. What Russian would not give you 15 to 20 minutes of their time? It's probably the one who is not going to be buying from you.

- An I-Plan is used to help managers look good. If your manager or user is an up and comer in the organization, they will appreciate an I-plan because it shows they were thorough, prepared, and had a strategic rather than just a tactical look at the project. It makes them look good to

Mr. J. Jones
Vice-President
ABC Company
123 Main Street
Anywhere, USA

SUBJECT: Implementation of Project XYZ

Dear Mr. Jones:

You and your assessment team have been working on selecting a vendor for your XYZ project. We have been told that you and your team will make a decision in a few weeks, and we would like to get together with you to discuss an executive implementation plan.

On any project like this, the first 30–90 days after implementation are crucial for you and your team to maximize the benefits and the ROI on the investment you are making. We have had experience with these types of projects and can identify for you what the key items are from both your team's and your selected vendor's perspective. We look forward to a brief meeting with you to identify at an executive level the key items you can keep track of during the implementation of project XYZ to maximize the investment you are making and minimize the amount of time it will take for you to start reaping the benefits of this solution.

Regards,

S. Smith
Sales Representative
M3 Learning

Figure 8-4. Sample I-Plan

their boss and also makes the boss look good to the organization.
- An I-Plan is a mutually beneficial document for transfer of ownership. It shows prospects their risks and what they should keep an eye on to minimize those risks, since risks can cost money. It helps you because it gives you insight into what is important to the senior execu-

tive and lets you assess how serious they are regarding your solution.

- An I-Plan can be used in the final closing step to ask for an order. As part of your proposal, it can be used to show your professionalism and thoroughness. It can incorporate the Implementation Date, which combined with your SalesMap lets you control the buy/sell process to which the prospect has already committed.

The I-Plan is a sales document positioned in between Validate and the final proposal that gives you information at a key juncture in the buy/sell process. It lets you test out the process you have gone through already, allows you access to senior managers to get their buy in, and sets the stage for you controlling the outcome of the final proposal.

A final note: The I-Plan and SalesMap are two of the most powerful tools in this book, but we have observed that, of the salespeople who have been through ProActive Selling, fewer than 30 percent actually implement these two tools. Why? The reason is they take some work. Unlike the Flip or Three Levels of Why tools, they require some actual preplanning and detailed work. Like anything else, the things that take the most time usually yield the biggest rewards. Use the tools.

Tool Drop, Push, Pull^Tool

It is now decision time, and the decision is yours to make. You have gotten to this stage by following a process, and with skills and tactics, you have arrived in a strong sales position. If you feel you are in a strong position, one where you believe you have a better than 50 percent chance of winning, you should SBP to the next step called Close. If you do not think you are in the best competitive position, you have three choices. You can:

1. Drop it: Any more time or effort by you is just throwing good resources after a bad situation.
2. Push to a Close: Pushing is not the most desirable option, but owing to time constraints, competitive pres-

sure, or the prospect wanting to make a decision ASAP, you may have to push. When you push you are out of control, so it usually costs you something, and it usually costs you money. You end up discounting, matching a competitive offering, or giving something away to get the order. Whatever it is, pushing a deal is risky, does not ensure a victory, and in the long and short run, costs you margin.

3. Pull: The third option is to go back and start pulling. Go back to the Educate process and start again to pull the prospect through the buy/sell process and create the value for your product or service. Going back through the Educate/Validate/Justify process is different for every sale. In some cases, it may take 5 minutes. In others, it may take 5 hours, five meetings, 5 days, 5 weeks, or 5 months. The point is, you have to go back and get control of the buy/sell process. If the prospects do not understand your solution and take ownership of it, they are not going to understand your price. If they do not understand your price, you have violated the Law of Value Creation.

THE LAW OF VALUE CREATION

If all things are equal, people will buy on price. The job of a ProActive salesperson is to create a value difference so prospects do not see things as equal, because they are not.

ProActive salespeople know that if all things are equal, and the prospect is deciding based on price, they have not done their job.

In the Justify phase, you are asking prospects to do something they hate doing and will avoid doing at all costs. You are asking them to change; and people for the most part hate to

Buy – Sell Process

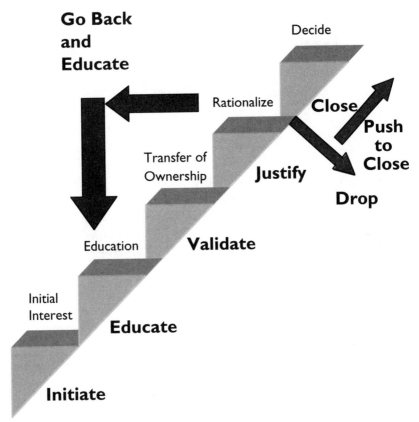

Figure 8-5. Pull/Go back to the Educate chart

change. Your best chance to finalize this sale is to stay the course. Stay with the strategies you started out with and have continued with during the entire process. By staying the course and using the tools described in this chapter, you will put yourself in the position of greatest return, and that return is the order.

Chapter 9

The Skill of Closing the Deal

You've done it. You have walked with the prospect through the buy/sell process, and you feel you are in the best competitive position you can be in. You have worked together with the prospect to develop a hard-hitting proposal, complete with an Implementation Plan and a SalesMap of all the activities you have done with them throughout the buy/sell process, and you are ready to proceed to the final step.

What Is a Close?

The close means something different to a prospect than it does to a salesperson. To a prospect, it is the final logical step in a business evaluation process. Prospects and their team have been involved every step of the way through an evaluation that will require an investment of resources to change a process within the organization. They also may be purchasing goods or service by themselves, and the need for a committee and a process may be minimal. In this case, the prospect has evaluated the need to invest resources, their own money, to change something: the car they drive, their appearance, the place they live, or where they will go on a vacation. Whatever the size or scope of the effort, the prospect sees this step as a decision, either yes or no. It's why it is called Decide on the Buyer side of the buy/sell process. They are now ready to make a decision.

A reactive salesperson views this step as the time to "close a deal." It's time to get ink on paper, bring it home, get a signature, a John or Jane Hancock, or whatever else you call getting the prospect to commit to your solution. A reactive salesperson sees this as time to get the order, chalk it up in the win column, and get paid. This is one-dimensional thinking.

The obvious problem is that the prospect and the salesperson are going into the final step with different agendas. With two different agendas, there is bound to be some confusion, and there are two different potential outcomes. The ProActive salesperson sees this final step just as the prospect sees it. It is a chance to make a decision. However, the prospect, in the eyes of the salesperson, has three choices, not two. The prospect can say yes, no, or maybe, where a maybe is anything that prevents a yes or no decision. A maybe could be competition, a delay, a move to table the decision to a higher source—anything that prevents a yes or no. Maybes are never good for a salesperson, since by definition, a maybe means the salesperson is not in control of the process.

So how can a salesperson control the final step? Just like in all the other steps. Control the process, and think like a buyer.

Define the Process

The art of closing can fill another book by itself. There are numerous negotiating tactics you can use in a sale that is in the closing phase to try to get an order.

- Good Cop, Bad Cop: One person takes the side of the customer and is very empathetic, and the other person is the "bad cop" and plays someone who is very hard to deal with.
- Split the Difference: The two sides in the negotiation are a set difference apart, and you agree to split the difference.
- Nibbling: Offer small increments of something. Give the customer a discount, then offer no sales tax, then give free delivery, then gift wrap it for free, and so on.

- Agree, Deflect, Agree: This is a tactic to move someone. "I agree with you Mr. Jones. Some people would also think this way, which I am sure you would agree would . . ."
- Puppy Dog: Take something and try it out. Like a puppy, once you get it "home," the odds of a return are minimal.
- Written Word: Once something is in writing, it is hard to argue with. Think when you shop for something at the shopping mall. Once something has a price tag on it, you rarely think of negotiating from that asking price.

There are many, many more negotiating tactics you can use in a closing situation to try to get the order. In ProActive Selling, you have already done all the hard work by controlling the process. It is now up to you to have the buyer make a yes or no decision, and you do this by working the process you have used already to get the sale to this point and by thinking like a buyer.

Use the Tools

You have many tools at your disposal that you can use to SBP this final meeting to a decision.

The 30-Second Speech

Start the meeting out with a 30-second speech: Introduction, three discussion points from the last meeting or the entire buy/sell process, three final issues or points, suggest the outcome of the meeting, gain agreement, then get into the agenda of the meeting.

30-SECOND SPEECH

"Good afternoon, and thank you for attending today's meeting. We have gone through a process over the last few months, and together we have determined that:

---

1. The need for a solution in this area is critical. We have documented the steps both of us have taken during this evaluation and arrived at a solution we are going to review today.
2. The solution you are evaluating from our company seems to do exactly what you want.
3. The budget for this expenditure has already been justified.

You also stated that you:

1. Need this solution immediately,
2. Are concerned about the delivery and ramp up time, since you want it up and running by the twenty-second of the month, and
3. You wanted to have two financial options presented to you at this meeting.

This is what we are here to talk about today, and if we have a successful meeting, we can get a 2-day head start by executing the agreement that is in the proposal today, or we can execute the agreement by Friday, as planned to meet your Implementation Date of the twenty-second. Is this your understanding of the meeting today?"

This is a 30-second speech to begin a Closing meeting. Other tools you will be using in this Closing meeting include the following.

Implementation Date

In the above example, you already know the prospect wants to have your solution up and running by the twenty-second. The focus of the sales person *must* be on what is important to the prospect, the Implementation Date and BBB, not the date of the signing of the contract.

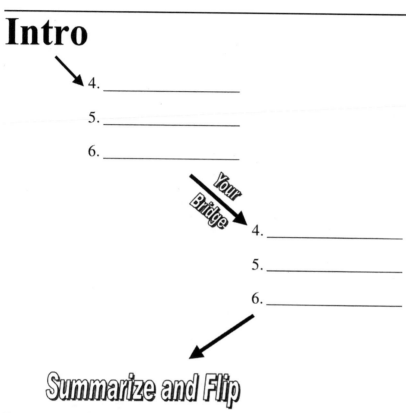

Figure 9-1. 30-Second Speech Worksheet

SalesMap

Your SalesMap is in the proposal so prospects can remind themselves how much work they have done to get to where they are
now. It helps overcome their fears.

> *"Have we done enough homework so we are comfortable*
>
> *with this change?"*
>
> *"Are we sure this is the best investment of our resources?"*
>
> *"Are we sure we can do this in the time required?"*

This is the process you and the prospect have gone through together, and it is a competitive advantage because you are probably the only vendor who has created a SalesMap with them.

Implementation Plan

This is also in your proposal, so the fear of the unknown is lessened. The SalesMap looks backward, and the I-Plan looks forward. Both of these tools will lower the prospect's perceived risk of change. The I-Plan allows the prospects to see what they should be doing in the first 30 to 90 days to maximize their return, improve the overall chance of success, and lessen the fear of the unknown.

The Three Languages

You will probably have managers (Spaniards), vice presidents (Russians), and even a president or CEO (Greek) in your final presentation. Remember to speak all languages, and when in doubt, always speak to a higher language; always speak up.

Three Levels of Why and Flipping

There probably will be some final questions. By now you know the most ineffective thing you can do is to answer these questions. Your job is not to answer questions first presented to you. Two rules of thumb are:

1. Senior executives ask a question only when they have a good idea of an answer, and
2. Your job is to get the real question/answer out, and you do that with Three Levels of Why, and Flipping.

Summarize, Bridge, and Pull

Summarize, Bridge, and Pull to the final step, and ask for the commitment and decision to start the process together. Make sure you emphasize the dragons. Satisfying these dragons are why they will make a decision.

Stay with this process, and use all the tools to start the meeting, run the meeting, and end the meeting in control of the process. Control the process, and you will win the sale. Prospects may try to wrestle control from you at the end of the final meeting by delaying making a decision on the agreed-to date. They may stall by deferring to another person not in the meeting or by introducing you to a new time schedule of which you were unaware. You still have your SBP tool, so you can get final control of the meeting, and adjust to any unforeseen circumstances or objections.

SBP: An Example of When You Have to Get Control Back

Example 1: The prospect has changed the decision date.

"Well, it seems we have had a good meeting. You have stated your desire to move ahead with the project. You still need it up by the twenty-second. Your manufacturing line needs to start on the twenty-fifth, or you will have heavy penalties to pay based on commitments you have made to your customers (Dragon). You cannot make a decision until Monday now, instead of this Friday, since the president will not be back in the office until then. You also said you have talked with him this week and expect no objections.

We have called our office and found out that if you commit on Monday, we can get everything ready and express ship to make your twenty-second date. Do you agree this is where we are?"

"Yes I do."

"Great, so we will be back here on Monday at 10:00 A.M. to finalize everything so we can make that date of the twenty-second." (Not pick up the order!)

Example 2: The prospects are getting nervous about the investment, and they want to wait.

"We have had a good meeting today. You have stated your desire to go ahead with this service, but now want to put it on hold. You are

comfortable with the solution, and the investment you are making relative to the return you are getting is well within the realm of acceptability, over $1 million within the first 12 months. You also wanted to make sure the project gets completed within 150 days from commencement of the project, which according to the I-Plan, both sides can commit to. Based upon the SalesMap and the I-Plan we have worked together on, your risks of this project delivering its proposed financial benefits of over $4 million over 3 years have been identified, and according to you, are acceptable (Dragon). We have stated our desire to move ahead and meet your schedule, so I think we have had a good meeting, is this correct?

"Yes, it has been a good meeting."

"Good. The next step is to look at the financial investment being made. If we can't agree to terms now, the risk increases as will the time to a solution. We need to figure out what we can do as a team to make this hold issue go away. Is this where we need to go as a next step?"

Just as with a price objection, you have to summarize the buy/sell process and the tools you have used, and attack ROI, time, and risk. If you let all things become equal, you need to go back and reeducate. If that still does not work, you are probably dealing with a manager who isn't the final decision maker. The only reason you would still be in a price situation is that you are out of control of the process. Drop, Push, or Pull; it's your choice.

The Real Art of Closing Is in the Definition: Think Like a Buyer

If there is one major theme in the closing meeting, it is to think like a buyer. In real life situations, as well as the role plays students go through in our classes, it is amazing how they get greedy at the end of the sale, think like a salesperson, and ask for the contract to be signed. It's not about you; it's about them; them, them, them. Stay in the prospect's perspective, and close the sales out by keeping the perspective on them. Remember the differences between thinking like a buyer and thinking like a seller:

Seller	Buyer
Contract signed	Implementation date
Cost	Return on investment
Price	Investment to get the return desired
Next step forward	Logical decision step
Ask for the order	Make a decision—yes or no
Get contract by end of the month	Make a decision—implementation date may be at risk

If you maintain your composure and stay the course of thinking like a buyer, you have the best opportunity to stay in control of this sale.

Celebrate Success

Finally, make sure you celebrate success with your new customer. You have done everything right and worked the tools in ProActive Selling to keep in control of the buy/sell process. ProActive salespeople make sure they:

1. Tell the buyers they did the right thing.
2. Express to them how pleased you are to have them as a customer.
3. Say when they can expect to hear from you next (SBP).
4. Wrap up professionally.
5. Don't oversell. ProActive salespeople take the order and leave.

Congratulations. You have followed the process, used all the right tools, and are a ProActive salesperson. You have made it through the process of ProActive Selling, and you should be thinking of how to use the tools and follow the process on all your prospects. ProActive Selling will improve your chances of getting a sale, increase the qualification skills you possess, and give you more tools for you to use at the point of attack, the sales call, than you ever had before.

Chapter 10

Applying the ProActive Selling Process

The Buy/Sell Process Reversed

You have spent most of your time with this book understanding how a buyer buys, thinking like a buyer to learn what tactics to use during a sales call. It is now time to think like a salesperson and ProActively figure out what to do with all this information. It is good to have added more tools to your sales toolbox, but now the questions you are asking are: Which one do I use when? How do I begin?

How to Start: Prepare

The first thing you need to do is get organized. While reading this book, you have probably, like all outstanding salespeople, started to apply some of the tools right away to current accounts, especially the ones that are in your Maybeland. You use a ProActive tool for one account, then remember another tool that could be used for another account, and before you know it, you have used a few tools; you then put the tools back on the shelf, never to remember them again.

Many managers who teach their sales team the ProActive Selling process find that teaching them once is not enough.

> "I learned so much the first time, but the second time
>
> through, I really took away so much more."

I wish salespeople could learn completely on the first go around, and they do learn, but repeated exposure to the tools will make salespeople more successful. You have to plan to use the tools first.

PowerHour was designed for you to focus on your Red-Zone accounts. Start with that. Figure out no more than three accounts you currently want to go after with your new set of tools. They may be ones that you are working on now, or all new prospects. Pick a manageable number, and focus on those.

During PowerHour, determine where in the process they are. Is the prospect in the Education phase? Has ownership transferred, and are you in Validate? Have you just started, and are you now planning your Initiate call? Plan out your sales call,

Ideas I can implement:

	IDEAS	TOOL TO BE USED	RESULTS EXPECTED
1			
2			
3			
4			
5			
6			
7			
8			
9			
10			

Figure 10-1. PowerHour action plan

determine what you want to accomplish, and then use the tools that apply. You need to have all the tools listed and available to you, or you will end up using two or three, and forgetting all the rest. Appendix A has a list of the Proactive Sales Tools for you to copy and post up in your office. It will remind you which tools are available to you to use at any given time.

The Second Step: Practice

Once you have started reviewing the tools, practice. Most people will start with a 30-second speech or a Summarize, Bridge, and Pull. Make sure you script out exactly what you want to do, and include the tools. Try to use them exactly as you have learned them here. It is really easy to do an *Intro–2–1* 30-second speech, and you'll feel good that you at least got one done. Stay with the program. A 30-second speech is *Intro–3–3–Summarize and Flip*. It will feel uncomfortable, but the person sitting across the desk or on the other end of the phone from you will love it. Practice makes perfect.

Design a SalesMap form. What would one actually look like? Use the computer and make up a sample one. Do not use the example in the book since ownership will not transfer. You have to do one from scratch.

What would an Implementation Plan look like? What would be useful for your specific sales situation? The sample I-Plan included in the book can be a good start, but try and make one up yourself. If you are having difficulty, go back to some of your current customers and ask them what was important to them during the first 30 to 90 days after they started the relationship with you. Most likely, what you thought was important to them and what they were actually measuring were different; they usually are.

The MMM questions are key. Come up with ways you can ask these questions, the earlier in the sales process, the better. All seven questions are important, and Implementation Date is on the top of the list.

Three Levels of Why is fun, but you really have to keep digging to get at the third level of why. Sarah Berry, who works for one of our clients, now claims she is so good at Three Levels of Why that, on a recent call, the prospect at the end of the call proclaimed,

> *"I have just told you more information than I should have and more information than I have told anyone else. I'm OK with that though because it has crystallized my thinking as well."*

This is a win–win if ever there was one.

Use all the tools, but only a few at a time. Change them week by week, adding some and dropping others. The more exposure you have to the tools, the more you will incorporate into your actual sales toolbox.

Have a support group in your office. Have an early morning meeting once or twice a week to practice what tactics you are going to use on your next few sales calls. Practice in front of your peers. This is a very hard thing to do, but it is important. If you are all alone or work from home, use the phone. Call others so they can critique and offer assistance. Remember, if one of your fellow sales team members asked you for help, you would offer your help in a second. Asking for help is not a sign of weakness; it is one of the toughest things salespeople can do, since they always think they are in control. Ask for help, and you will be amazed at how quickly you incorporate the tools into your daily sales processes.

The Third Step: Implement the Process

Now that you have learned to use the tools individually, it is time to map out the process. Remember to master the tools first, then the process. This does sound a little backwards, because you are probably used to learning the process first, then the tools. Learning how to sell is like learning anything else, one step at a time. When you learned how to play a musical instrument, it was notes first, then the chords. With sports, learning to drive, or learning how to walk, you started one step at a time.

Then the bigger issues become manageable. The same is true with ProActive Selling; learn the individual tools first.

Once you have started mastering the tools, you can look at the process. There is a process in how people buy, and you need to match these steps to the buyers' steps. Begin with your current accounts, and map the ProActive Selling Process to where you are with the account. A good way to look at the process is to develop a ProActive Process Selling Sheet such as that shown in Figure 10-2.

This is a simple selling sheet, and you can automate it in Excel or any other spreadsheet program so you can keep track of your deals. When you become good at it, you will be able to use this sheet to:

- Follow the right process. It is very easy to get lost in a sale. You must stay focused on the buy/sell cycle. There are three types of "process sellers" out there, and being ProActive is going to make you more successful than any of the three.
  - *Proposal Sellers* think that by skipping the Educate and Validate steps, they are closer to the close of a sale. These are the most confused salespeople since they gear up for selling a proposal. They start with Initiate and get the prospect initially interested. Then they think, since they have an "interested" prospect, they should just sell a proposal. The proposal has all the relevant information in it, and once the prospect "sees" the value solution in the proposal, they should sign right away. Prospects won't. The proposed solution has no value to the prospect, since there has been no education and transfer of ownership of the value as there has been for your solution. Using this process, you will have to discount to match the prospect's "budget" or competitive offers.
  - *Demo Sellers* are busy selling demos. They believe their job is to get the prospect in front of the solution as soon as possible. Once they see this "thing" perform, they will "see" the value and have to buy. Demo sellers go past the education phase so fast, prospects have

ProActiveSelling

Account Name _____

Names of Contacts	Titles	Phone	E-mail	Buyer Level

Sales Description

_____

Sales Process

	Initial Interest	Education	Demonstration	Validate	Close
Completed Dates					

Buying Situation: What is going on? _____

MMM Qualification

What is the "process" to obtain funds? _____

What is the implementation date?

← ——— Pull vs. Push? ——— →

Fill in dates and tasks above.

What is the backwards decision process?   Start with implementation date. _____

What is the Buying Criteria?

Product Features _____

Product Quality _____

1

Figure 10-2. Excel Selling Sheet

no opportunity to understand fully what the salesperson is offering. They get it, but do not really get it. They get what your solution is, but do not get WIIFT. The Law of Creating Value says if all things are equal, prospects will buy on price. Selling demos

Professional Support/Ease of Use _____

_____

Investment _____

_____

Image _____

_____

Is there a need? _____

Can we meet the needs? _____

What are the top 2 "client spoken" benefits? _____

WINS - All Levels

Institutional Reason _____

_____

_____

Individual Reason _____

_____

_____

Figure 10-2. Excel Selling Sheet (Continued)

allow the prospect to see all solutions as equal, since they have not had the opportunity to understand your solution fully, and therefore your price difference. With demo selling you again will have to push to make the sale.

- *ProActive Process Sellers* are the salespeople who know they have to take the selling process one step at a time, since that is how buyers buy. Skipping steps will allow the prospect to gain control, which is not a good thing. The buy/sell process can take 5 minutes, or 5 hours, 5 days, 5 weeks, or however long your sales process needs to take. It is guaranteed that if you do follow the buy/sell process, you can control the deal since you have the tools to be in control. The bottom line is that you will close more deals using a process. They will

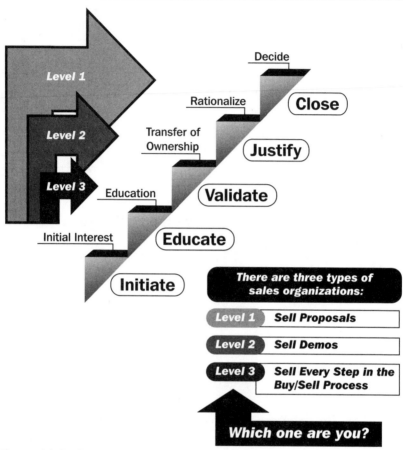

Figure 10-3. Selling process diagram

close faster, you will be in control, and you will avoid Maybeland.

- Stay longer in the early steps of the buy/sell process. Using Figure 10-2, you will be able now to use the Educate process to make sure your product fit and qualification questions are answered. You will also be able really to understand the prospect's questions. Education is a two-way process. Spend a good amount of time educating the prospect. Then you can use the Validate step to reinforce the education process, rather than using the Validate step to educate. This is a common mistake. It does seem the longer you stay in the education stage, the better off you are, so stay there as long as you think you need to, and do not have the prospect push you forward at a pace that will decrease your chances for a sale. Once you pass the education stage, the buy/sell process starts to take off, activity levels increase, and the prospect is starting to gear up for a decision. The more homework you have done, the better you can create value in the later part of the process.

• Stay in control. Prospects are going to want to map out their process near the end of the sale and have you follow it, especially the more senior the executive, or the higher the dollar value of the sale. Using the selling sheet in Figure 10-2 you will be able to stay in control. The closer to the end you are, the greater the pressure for control of the process. You need to avoid the reactive selling mistake: As you get closer to the end of a sale, you end up thinking,

> *"If I do what the prospect is asking for, I'll get the sale."*

Remember this from Chapter 1? Following and controlling the process will allow you to have valid business reasons for countering the prospect's desire to control the process.

• Know when you have a qualified deal. Unless the MMM questions are answered, you should not be going past the Education stage. If you have a process sheet in front of you, are entering the Validate phase, and you still have four of the seven MMM questions unanswered, Maybeland is coming up really fast. As stated before, it is our experience that if you master the seven questions of MMM, you will do more to affect your income than anything else covered in this book.

- Use the ProActive Selling Process Sheets to create your Implementation Plan. This is a perfect document to provide input to an I-Plan. Prospects have a tendency to forget all the things they have done with you in earlier steps; the history becomes a blur. Using this process sheet to remind them of the value and the hard work you have mutually done to date will give your I-Plan a competitive advantage.

Keep your process sheets simple. The worst thing to do is come up with something so complex you will tire of using it. Selling process sheets should go into your WarBooks, which you should be looking at during PowerHour, and so on. Create a new behavior and stick with it. Twenty-five qualification questions, or pages and pages of diagrams and organizational maps serve only one purpose: They keep you busy doing internal instead of external activities. You need to concentrate instead on external activities and keep prospecting.

The Fourth Step: Get Them Involved

Now comes the fun part. When you get really good at process sheets and fitting them in your WarBooks, you can enlist the prospect to help you in the process. Many ProActive salespeople share their WarBooks or at least the buy/sell process with the prospect. It works very well at the managerial level, and when you call on upper level management, it acts as a tool that keeps you in control of that sales call as well. Since it is all about them, they get very interested.

Get creative. Have a part in your WarBook that the prospect has to fill out. Give that prospect a copy, and make sure you both bring your copies to the meetings. The more you can use the sales process sheets to transfer ownership, the better off you are.

An executive overview section in the WarBook for some of your larger deals is appropriate as well. This is where you document the Value (ROI, time, risk, motivation, and brand) issues, document the value-based reasons for the Russian on why they want to become more competitive, and then identify how your solution can help them. If also expressed in financial terms, there will be some gaps, missing numbers, or ROI information the senior person will want to help in filling out.

Have WarBook meetings. Remember the GETS chart? Have GETS meetings, which would include WarBook reviews, SalesMap discussions, and good discussions around the MMM questions, especially the process ones. This is a great way to have progress reports and ensure that both parties are still involved. It helps with the transfer of ownership, and every so often, you can invite a senior manager to sit in.

The Fifth Step: Share with Others

If want to get really good at the tools in ProActive Selling, teach. Share what you do and what you are going to do with others. Share your current ideas, and put them together in a 15-minute presentation. What tools are you using, and how are you customizing the tools to use them better? There are four levels of salespeople.

At the first level is the rookie salesperson, the one just starting out. The second level salesperson is the one who has been around for a few years, has some experience, has been through some training, and has had some successes and failures. Third level salespeople are very good. They are the ones who are very perceptive based on their knowledge, experience, and talents. Most top salesleaders in organizations are perceptive salespeople. At the very top are the fourth level salespeople. They are the ones who can teach. They understand what they do so well and have taken ownership of the tools they use so well that they can teach them to others. This fourth level salesperson has the confidence to go into almost any situation and come out winning, because they have a clear mastery of selling tools. They got that mastery by teaching others.

The same holds true with the tools in ProActive Selling. Once a week, once a month, seek out someone and tell that person how you are using a tool, or how you are going to use one, and why. Do not make the mistake of explaining how you used a tool. Past discussions are great, but in teaching the tools, you

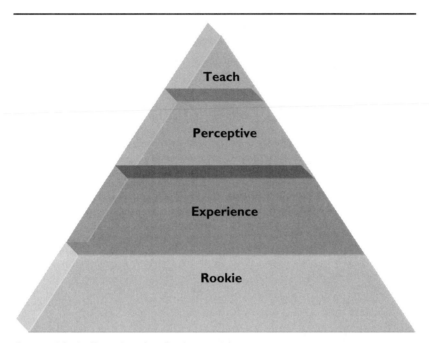

Figure 10-4. Four levels of salespeople

want to put yourself out there and discuss the unknown, current deals you can affect. History discussions can be used to validate the education of the selling tools. Use current discussions to teach and past examples to have the learning really sink in.

Teach the tools, share them with others, and you will find yourself taking ownership of these tools and developing new tools that are tailored to your own situation. You probably need more tools in your toolbox than just your current hammer and drill anyway, and if you can share your new tools with others, you will become a master at using them.

The Languages

Over and over, the languages concept is the one salespeople really get an ah-ha! from. Salespeople understand they need to call high and stay high. The problem is their company is putting out *Feature/Function* sales and marketing tools for them to use. Marketing collateral, demos, proposals, trade shows, selling tools, everything is designed for a salesperson to master *Feature/Function* selling. When salespeople get together, their common language is Spanish. Sales account reviews done with sales management are also done in Spanish. Everyone has a common language, Spanish. There just is too much Spanish.

You can, of course, tell the Marketing department as well as all departments about the three languages and the need for more selling assistance to speak in terms of value (Russian and Greek). You probably should do this to effect change. Instead of throwing grenades at everyone else, you can do something yourself. Teach them. You can take the initiative, master the languages, and help the organization speak all three. Tips for getting better at the three languages include using:

- PowerHour: When you are in PowerHour, focus your homework on the seven WarBook questions. The War-Book questions are a financial look at your prospects. Try to understand why EPS is so important. Read the annual report and find out how the senior executives are being compensated. You probably can bet their compensation has some ties to the goals and strategies they are giving the people who work for them.
- Current Customers: Call on current customers. Talk to the CFO, VP of Sales, or other executives within your current customers' organizations. Since you are currently a vendor, they will usually grant you some time, as long is there is something in it for them. Talk to them about how your product or service is working in their account, and ask for their opinion on how they could be using it better, to maximize their ROI. Get the meeting and listen; *do not pitch.* This is not selling time; this is learning a language time. You can use what you will be learning later. Remember, if you are getting a meeting to learn a new language, say Russian, and in return you converse with the executive in Spanish, the chances of you getting any more

meetings with this Russian are slim to none. Learn a language, and try to talk back to the executive in the same language, and leave the sales pitch back at the office.

- Homework: There are important things you should be reading: outside periodicals, prospects' financial statements, *The Wall Street Journal,* annual reports, the financial section of the prospect's Web site, and so on. Become a student of Value—their value. You know you are becoming successful when your desk has financial reports and documents about your prospect's business rather than your own marketing collateral.

- Prospecting Calls: Develop a 30-second pitch for upper level management. It seems that 90+ percent of salespeople say that they want to call high in an organization. They are being told to, and they do, but then they have an expectation of being passed down to a manager. It is acceptable to the reactive salesperson to be passed down.

> *"The top executive told me what to do, and now*
>
> *I can reference the top executive when I call the*
>
> *lower level person. They will have to take my call."*

The two things that need to be fixed in this scenario are:

  1. Change the paradigm. Reward yourself for successful senior management calls differently than for manager calls. It cannot be an acceptable practice for you to be passed down. It should make you angry, since you now know what to say to senior management.

  2. Change the 30-second speech. Most 30-second speeches are focused on what the seller can offer the buyer. Remember, they do not care about you; they care about themselves. Prospect with WIIFM in the 30-second speech.

- Focus: Stay the course. Keep mastering all languages, and you will find yourself becoming multilingual. Homework you do will now appear to you in a multilingual format. Homework is always presented in multiple languages; you just have to learn how to read in a multilingual way.

An Example of a Multilingual Story

Here is a fictitious newspaper article. Look how it is written in three languages, and watch how your interest shifts.

Layoffs in the Recording Industry

> Spanish Introduction

LOS ANGELES - Struggling music power Tip-Top Records said yesterday that it will slash about 30 percent of its nearly 7,200-person workforce and dump about 200 acts from its roster in an effort to improve profits during an industry wide slump.

"There are some real challenges facing the music industry at the moment," Tip-Top CEO Jim Bertram says. "However, we are firmly on target to improve Tip-Top's performance, and we are optimistic about our ability to attack larger issues."

Tip-Top—whose hitmakers include Steve W., John Brown, and superstar Christina M.—has been hurt as U.S. album sales in 2001 fell nearly 5 percent.

> Some Spanish and Russian mixed in. Stills hold your interest.

Tip-Top's market share slid when it didn't have a hit to rival its release in late 2000 of The Early Rock and Roll Days. Superstar Gordon Loss failed to sparkle when his album *Funny* ended up selling only 400,000 copies. In January the company agreed to pay him $35 million to end their four-album contract.

> Good Spanish. Borders on gossip, which is real heavy duty Spanish.

Tip-Top is the No. 6 record company in the United States, with 11.3 percent of album sales so far in 2002, down from 14.2 percent in the same period last year, according to Soundscan.

In search of a turnaround, Tip-Top in October recruited Bertram, who had spiffed up Capital before Bertelsmann bought it in 1999.

> Here comes the real Russian and Greek. By this time, Spaniards are losing interest in the story, since they got the gossip points already, while the Russians and Greeks are just starting to get involved.

Now, Bertram predicts higher market share and better cash-flow margins as Tip-Top cuts costs, embraces new distribution technology, including DVDs and the Web, and attacks piracy.

The cuts should save $130 million a year by 2005, he says, and margins could grow in three years to 12 percent from the 2.1 percent expected this year.

Bertram will focus on marketing Tip-Top's best known labels, DeLux and GoldOne, and stars. "Not having star power tends to take the margins out of the music and makes it a commodity," he told analysts in Los Angeles. That's one reason Tip-Top plans to drop more acts. "We've cut the artist roster a lot, but it was still pretty bloated," he says.

Several analysts were impressed with the changes. "The size of the cost savings beat our expectations, and the margin improvement is ahead of what we were looking for," says CreditSwiss analyst Hank Bush. "It's the turnaround story of the media sector." Still, Merrill Lynch's Ron Lewis says Tip-Top's ability to achieve its cash-flow goals "depends on a recovery (in music) and breaking more acts in the United States. But the team they put together is very compelling."

Tip-Top shares were up nearly 3 percent in U.S. trading.

Learn to read and understand all languages. The Multilingual Story is an example of how you have to focus on all languages in a story, not just what makes the headlines. It might be more interesting to read and talk Spanish, but Russians and Greeks make the decisions.

Chapter 11

Managing the ProActive Selling Process

Sales management, this chapter is for you. *ProActive Selling* is a book on the tactics of selling within a process. It is not *the* way to sell or a high level strategic approach to selling.

Since it focuses on tactics before strategies within a process, you can coach and council to specific actions and can measure improvements. The skills of selling are teachable, and it is your job as a sales manager to make sure your sales team and the culture of your sales organization are in a learn and grow mode. Top salespeople want to be in a "learn and grow" organization, since that is what they desire most and excel in. If they can learn and grow, the income associated with being in a learn and grow organization will follow. In this spirit, the tools *ProActive Selling* offers fit sales management's coaching skills very well.

In *ProActive Sales Management*, managers were given tools to get their job done. Now it is time to use some of the tools that were defined in that book and apply them to managing the ProActive Sales Process.

Tool-Based Selling

As you have read, *ProActive Selling* has 20 tools that salespeople must master. The truth is, as in most strategy-based sales training efforts, salespeople attempt three or four different things and then over time forget the rest. This is not a very effective approach in changing sales behavior.

Since ProActive Selling is not purely strategy based, you as the manager do not have to get involved with the strategy of an account to work the tools and dramatically increase performance.

Look at what a typical sales manager does on a daily basis. A sales manager will digest sales forecasts and answer far too many voice mails and e-mails. After an entire day of being reactive, the manager may have some time to be ProActive. The manager would love to get close to some of the deals the salespeople are working on, so in some spare moments, the manager does one or two of the following things:

- Goes over Account Strategy on hot accounts with the sales team.
- Critiques sales strategy.
- Has Quarterly Reviews with a sales account focus.
- Goes on sales calls and listens to the entire call, then adds subjective feedback.
- Goes on sales calls and gives "objective" feedback.

The questions now are: What benefit have you really provided? Have you provided your sales expertise, or extensive sales knowledge? Do you remember when you were a salesperson? How much did your manager add value?

You now have the ability to change this paradigm. You have a way to create a ProActive sales culture, and you do it thorough the tools.

Tool $R = F + C^{Tool}$ **and** M^2O/t^{Tool}

In *ProActive Sales Management*, there is a discussion of how if you are managing to revenue alone, you are managing to the wrong thing. You need to be ProActive and measure the things that make up revenue, which are frequencies and competencies. If salespeople do a lot (increase their frequency) of good things (competencies), revenue will happen. To be a step ahead, sales managers need to manage to the formula $R = F + C$, revenue equals frequencies plus competencies, and focus on the *F*s and *C*s, not just the *R*.

The way a good sales manager can implement frequencies and competencies is to focus on *M²O/t: Mutually beneficial Measurable Objectives over Time*. To be successful in implementing any process, not just a sales process, objectives must be set so they can be measured. The only objectives that are going to get done are the ones to which both parties agree, which is the mutual part. Objectives must also be measured over a time constraint, which brings you back to *M²O/t*. By using *M²O/t*s, you as a manager can measure salespeople against your level of expectations, especially on the use of the tools presented in *ProActive Selling*.

Any process or tool that you are going to implement has to be accepted by the sales team. *M²O/t* will allow you the flexibility to focus on the tools you need to focus on at any given time. Which tools do you need to focus on? That brings up the next topic of the SOS Pyramid.

Tool The SOS Pyramid™

How do you know where to start when you implement ProActive Selling as a tool in your organization? Welcome to the SOS Pyramid.

The SOS Pyramid is a starting tool for sales managers to plan their tactical and strategic objectives. The base of the Pyramid is for you to do a *situational analysis*. What is your selling process like now, and what are the pros and cons to it? What do you do well that you want to leverage, and what needs improvement? What tools need to be implemented first, second, and third? Do a situational analysis to determine where you and your sales team currently are at.

The first thing you will probably deduce in your SOS Pyramid is the overall requirement to set up the buy/sell process for your organization. Get everyone inside and outside of sales to commit to the idea that you and your team will now be using a process to sell. Communicate to everyone that the process your team is going to be using will be the process for the company. Successfully implementing the buy/sell process into the sales

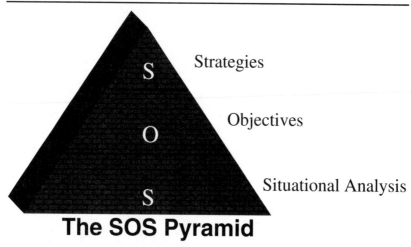

The SOS Pyramid

Figure 11-1. The SOS Pyramid

team and beyond will allow everyone to communicate within the organization effectively. It will give you a common vocabulary and allow communication within the sales team and between different departments within the company to transpire in the language of the sales team and the customer.

Then, use the Pyramid to establish what specific tools in ProActive Selling are needed the most right now. Determine your immediate needs from your situation analysis, and then set M^2O/ts with your salespeople. Is your main focus right now on prospecting skills? The 30-second speech and the Summarize, Bridge, and Pull tools should be at the top of your list. Is it major account development that needs work? The SalesMap and Implementation Plan would be a great fit. If you have too many maybes in the funnel, the MMM questions should be of immediate importance. Ascertain what your top sales objectives are right now, set your *Strategy,* and for the next 3 to 6 months, match the tools of ProActive Selling to what you are trying to do as a sales team to become more productive.

Finally, the Pyramid is an effective way to help you change the M^2O/ts as often as you want to. Do a Pyramid once a quarter to determine what M^2O/ts can come off and be replaced by new ones, as well as which ones need to stay on and be reinforced. By adding a bit of structure to your implementation of ProActive Selling, you will be assured that the right tools will be in the salesperson's bag at the right time.

| Tool | **The Miller 17^{Tool}** |

You need to put your M^2O/ts, the SOS Pyramid, your Frequencies and Competencies, and the tools of ProActive Selling all together. The Miller 17 is a way for you to communicate objectively the goals you want each salesperson to attain. It is a way for the top salespeople in your organization to know exactly what they need to do to become more successful, and for the mid and bottom level salespeople to know exactly what is expected of them to improve performance.

As you can see, the Miller 17 tracks three variables: Revenue, Frequencies, and Competencies. If you have your salespeople focused on the F and C, the R will adjust accordingly, since R is the reactive measure of the other two.

The Way to Interpret a Miller 17

In the example in Figure 11-2, take a look at each salesperson. For salesperson 1, the revenue lines look below normal. Now as a sales manager, what do you do?

> *"Selling is a numbers game. Need to make more sales calls."*

> *"Prospect, prospect, prospect is my motto."*

> *"Field time is revenue time."*

These are all true statements, but do they apply to salesperson 1? If you look at the frequencies, you can tell that this person is out in the field trying to drum up business, which is why a 5 ranking is seen in some of the frequencies. If you look at the competencies, however, this person needs help in product knowledge and SBP. As a manager, you now know what variables to focus on to increase revenue.

Second Quarter Reviews

1–5 Scale (1 = Low - 5 = Excellent)

PERFORMANCE	2.2	3.4	2.4	3.4	3.4
SALES Y-T-D	2	3	3	4	4
SALES QUARTER REVIEW	2	3	2	4	2
NEW SALES	3	2	1	3	5
RETENTION SALES	2	4	4	3	2
MARGIN SALES	2	5	2	3	4
SALES COMPETENCY	**2.8**	**4.2**	**2.2**	**3.5**	**4.2**
SALES CYCLE CONTROL	3	4	2	2	5
30-SECOND SPEECH	3	4	2	4	3
I-PLANS	3	5	2	2	4
PRODUCT KNOWLEDGE	2	3	4	5	4
SUMMARIZE/BRIDGE/PULL	2	5	2	3	4
WARBOOKS	4	4	1	5	5
FREQUENCY	**4.0**	**3.3**	**2.2**	**2.8**	**4.7**
MMM QUESTIONS ANSWERED	2	3	2	4	5
POWERHOURS	4	2	1	2	4
TIME DEMOS	3	3	4	3	4
FORECASTS BUY/SELL UPDATED	5	4	2	3	5
FIELD TIME MAXIMIZATION	5	4	2	2	5
CALLS PER WEEK	5	4	2	3	5

Figure 11-2. Sample Miller 17 for ProActive Selling

Looking at salesperson number 2, you find a different story. In this case, the salesperson's revenue is fine, and so are the competencies. If you look at the frequencies, you can tell there is a storm coming. This is a classic case of a salesperson focusing on a few deals that all come in at the same time, having nothing left in the funnel, and not yet getting hungry enough to go back out and prospect. By showing this person your frequency metrics, you and the salesperson can have a positive discussion about where this person needs to focus his or her time. Good salespeople will thank you for being so objective.

Finally, with salesperson number 3, you have a problem. Revenue is marginal; they are just barely holding on. The frequency and competency skills are lacking. This person may not make it, but you are working with this person to show what he or she specifically needs to do to get back on track. It is now up to the other person. You have done what you can, and now it is time to go focus on your A players and make them A+ players.

What you need to do with a Miller 17 is to sit down and establish your *F* and *C* metrics. What do you want to measure your sales team on when it comes for them to do a lot of good things? Some examples:

Frequencies	*Competencies*
Number of calls/week	Sales cycle control
Number of calls to Russians	Speaking all three languages
Proposals/month	30-Second speeches
PowerHour time	MMM questions
Selling time	Summarize, Bridge, and Pull
RedZone time	Product knowledge
Prospecting time	Sales strategy knowledge
Number of I-Plans/month	Three Levels of Why usage

These are just a few of many you can choose from. Pick the ones that you feel your organization needs now and will need over the next 3 to 6 months. What do you want them to do more of, and less of? When you answer this, develop your *F*, *C*, and *R* metrics. The *R* metric is easy, and the Miller 17 shows some that have been used before.

Now that you have your metrics, it is time to develop your scale. In the example above, it is on a 1 to 5 scale, with:

5: Way above expectations
4: Right on expectations
3: Just below expectations
2: Issues and concerns
1: Deficiencies

Now that you have your scale, go ahead and rank your sales team. How have they done, *R*, and what do you want them to do, $F + C$. Assign numbers to their efforts, and then communicate them to the sales team. You now have a document that you can manage to and use to ensure that the tools and tactics of ProActive Selling are going to be used and not forgotten. The following are some useful hints on implementing and using the Miller 17:

- Call it whatever you want. Unless your name is Miller, call it something else—the Smith 15, the Thomas 18, the Ishida 12. You get the picture. Try to have between 10 and 20 variables. Fewer than 10 are not worth doing. If you have more than 20, salespeople will not really know what to focus on.
- Not everyone is on the same scale. Your top performers should not get all 4s and 5s. Give out what your *expectations* are of the person, not how he or she ranks against his or her peers. An A+ performer can get a 2 or a 1 on a 30-second speech, even if it is the best one because it's your scale and it is based on your expectation of where you expect their level of proficiency should be, not where their proficiency is today.
- Don't be nice, be firm and fair. There's no use to giving out all 4 and 5 marks to make everyone happy. Be firm, and go with your gut instinct. Too many managers put down better scores to avoid conflict. You are masking issues by doing this, and you are not really helping anyone, including yourself.
- Insert ProActive Selling tools in competencies or frequencies. The Miller 17 is an obvious place to put ProActive Selling tools as well as the buy/sell process. Coaching from the Miller 17 ensures consistency for the entire team, and will extend the life of the tools.
- Alone or team approach. You can take your Miller 17, assign the values for the R, F, and C variables, then present it to each member; you can have a one-on-one session with the salesperson and complete it together; or you can fill one out, they can fill one out, and then you can have a joint discussion. All implementation strategies are effective; just use the one you feel will be most proactive.

- Do it now. Over the past ten years, the list of reasons why you should wait to implement a Miller 17 is pretty long.

    "Nice concept, and I'll do it at the start of the next quarter."

    "I have to wait for the next major sales meeting."

    "I have it in my head, and I'll find time when we do reviews in a few months."

    You know what happens then. Interruptions, new fires to put out, C players pounding at your door. The good ideas get put on the back shelf, since you are forced into being reactive again. Sales managers who have implemented a Miller 17 see their results soar. The A players grow faster than ever before. The C players are put on notice. The B players know what they have to do to move up. Sales managers have a focus now within their team, since everyone now knows specifically what is expected from them.

Developing a Miller 17 will give you a way to implement, monitor, and extend the learn-and-grow philosophy of your sales team. It provides a ProActive communication tool between management and salespeople on what needs to be done to be successful, and it is a mutually beneficial coaching vehicle. Implement one now, or go ahead, keep doing what you are doing, which will get you reactive results that will not be keeping up with your own high standards.

Sales Reviews: The Seven Questions

For managers, here is the real value of ProActive Selling. Here is where sales managers can be the most effective and be of the most value to their salespeople. The seven MMM qualifying

questions will have a greater effect on your sales team than anything else in this book. Becoming a master at the seven questions will give you a different perspective than the salesperson
has towards the account and even have them questioning their
own strategies and tactics in the account.

Money

1. *What is the process—to obtain a decision and to obtain a budget?*

Method

2. *What is the Implementation Date?*
3. *What are the steps in the buy/sell process?—Buyers Buy Back-wards (BBB)*
4. *What is the Decision Criteria? (PPPII)*

Motivation

5. *Is there a need?*
6. *Can you meet that need?*
7. *What are the top two prospect stated reasons? Why would they buy or implement your specific solution?*
   Three Levels of Why

On the surface, these seem like good qualifying questions
that all good salespeople should know. For a manager, they are
a powerful coaching set of tools.

Let's look at a typical account review. Your salesperson is in
the middle of a good size sale and feels good about the sales process to date. They are cautiously optimistic about the chances to
get this deal, and you have asked for the weekly, monthly, or
quarterly review of account activity. The salesperson has prepared an account overview for your review. It includes:

- The name of the account
- The people who are involved in the sale
- What has been the progress to date
- Where the situation is currently

- What they are going to be doing next and why
- Competitive issues
- Past account history, if there is any
- Strategic advantages you have
- What you are offering
- When this account is going to close
- The probability of success

This seems like a good list of items to have for an account review, and there are many more issues that are usually discussed. Each account takes 20 minutes or so to review, and both the salesperson and the sales manager feel good that they have discussed all pertinent issues, so on to the next account.

Now though, you as the ProActive sales manager can be more effective than you have ever been before. You now possess the power of the MMM questions. A typical review should now proceed like this:

"John, that was a good review. It sounds like we have done a good job to date, and we are on track to close this sale inside of 30 days."

"Yes, that is how I see it too, but it still is a competitive sale, and anything can happen."

"Agreed, but it looks good."

"I have placed it at better than an 85 percent chance of closing."

"Very good. I do have a few more questions before we move on."

"Sure, go ahead."

"John, what is the process to obtain a decision in this account?"

"The Director, Phil Howard, is making the decision."

"I didn't ask who. I asked what is the process they are using to make a decision? What other people are involved, and what is the process they are using to arrive at a decision? What is the step-by-step path it is going to take, who is it touching, and what is the final process in their buy decision?"

"Well, I haven't asked them all that since Phil said he was the one making the decision."

"Well, we had better find out. What is the process to obtain budget for a solution like this?"

"They have $50,000 budgeted for this."

"That's nice, but I didn't ask you how much they have budgeted. Russians give Spaniards budgets. Russians can do a lot with budgets, especially adding to them if the ROI is compelling. All this reconfiguring you are doing to stay within their 'budget' may not be needed if we know their process to obtain budgetary funds. Our initial solution for them was $75,000 before we started hacking it to make a budget number. We may want to test that out on the Russian as soon as possible."

"Good point."

"John, what is the Implementation Date?"

"I know that one. They have said they will get us an order by the end of the month."

"Again, that's good, but I didn't ask that question. I asked what date have they told you they want and need to start

implementing our solution. What date do they have to go live, have it on their desk, up and running?"

"Soon after they sign the order doesn't count, does it? I haven't asked. I have been so busy focusing on the contract signing date, I forgot about their date."

"That's easy to do. So if we do not have their Implementation Date, we cannot know their steps in the buy/sell process going backwards, can we?"

The conversation between management and salesperson takes on a whole different perspective. If the salesperson cannot answer most if not all of the MMM questions, do you really have a qualified prospect? Maybeland is right around the bend.

If the sales manager can master the MMM questions, salespeople will see the manager as adding value, salespeople will be working on only qualified selling situations, and forecast accuracy will increase dramatically. Implement the MMM questions as a part of your sales culture today.

Languages: The Manager's Value-Add

Sales management can be of a huge value to their salespeople by mastering all three languages. Salespeople understand the concept of all three languages, but have a tough time trying to stay fluent in Russian and Greek. Salespeople tend to gravitate to the lowest level of selling, the *Feature/Function* level because:

- It is what they have grown up with.
- Most if not all current marketing literature, sales literature, slides, and overheads are in Spanish, and stress *Feature/Function*.
- Most of their current contacts speak Spanish, and therefore there is no real drive to change.

- They rationalize they are doing fine, and they believe they can speak high-level languages when they need to. The question is: Will they seek out the need to meet with Russians and Greeks, or stay in their comfort zone?
- It's something new and requires change; people dislike change.

This is a perfect time for sales management to step in. You know multiple languages already. You routinely face:

- Budget issues
- Quota issues
- Hiring decisions
- Whether to send a salesperson on a sales trip
- Asking yourself if the cost of doing so is worth the revenue and earnings the trip will produce

You ask yourself more Russian questions than you give yourself credit for, since one of your hats, by definition, is to be a Russian. Your goal now is to become fluent in Revenue/Cost, ROI, and Market Share/Market Size issues, so you can coach and council your sales team also to master the three languages. The benefits of this are obvious.

1. You are a valuable resource. You have something salespeople recognize and will use, once they get access to a high level within their prospect's organization. Too many good salespeople will not take their boss on a sales call, since the only thing the boss knows how to do is act like a salesperson, and quite frankly, good salespeople believe they are better. They probably are, since they do it every day, and have been successful at it. You need to act like a manager, so speak like a manager, and help your good salespeople gain entry into the top levels of their top prospects.
2. Your salespeople will learn from you. You can actually teach them something, since you are now a master of all three languages, and have something they can learn.

3. Your top salespeople will call you more. Because you have this valuable tool, top salespeople will want you more often. Your past motto of:

> *"I just let my A+ salespeople run on their own. If*
>
> *they need me, they know I'll help them out, but*
>
> *quite frankly, they do not need as much help as my*
>
> *B and C salespeople."*

will go away. If this is something you would say, you need to do two things. One, go out and buy *ProActive Sales Management,* since you are much too reactive as a sales manager. Two, understand that if you do not develop skills top salespeople can use during senior sales situations, they will view you as a B or C level sales manager, since these are the people you are spending most of your time with.

4. The C level salespeople cannot dominate your time anymore. Your calendar, which is so full right now because of your needy C performers who are having you do their job for them, will open up. You will not want to go on sales calls with Spaniards, and since this is the call the C player prefers, you now have a right not to go on these calls that the C players should be handling themselves. In addition, if a C performer starts getting appointments at higher levels in their prospects and really needs you, is he or she really a C performer? It takes a fair degree of sales ability to get a meeting at higher levels of the organization, and this may be a way for C level salespersons to start to grow and improve their selling competencies.

5. Deals will qualify faster and close faster. This is obvious, since you are now at higher levels of decision making, where the MMM questions really work well and decisions are made faster.

6. You will be learning and growing. You will be in a situation where you are learning and growing, since learning all languages will be stretching yourself. It's about time you started to learn something new rather than just using the experience you have gained over the years.

7. You will be changing the sales culture of the organization. The more you learn the languages, the more successful you will become. You will be able to influence other sales teams, other departments, new sales collateral, management decisions regarding new products, and product launches. The three languages give you a perspective that not many others in the organization possess, a perspective which will enable you to see things from all aspects, which is very ProActive.

You can also change some of your sales management practices. Change the reward paradigms—reward yourself and your team differently for Russian calls than for Spanish calls. It should be an acceptable practice for your team to never be passed down to lower levels within the prospect's organization. It should make them angry, since they are gearing up for higher level selling situations and they know what to say to senior management. Instill in them the confidence to go on Russian and Greek sales calls alone. Set those expectations high.

How can you learn these languages? Do your homework. Read *Barron's, The Wall Street Journal, Investors Business Daily,* and other publications that senior managers read. Get on the Web and read your salespeople's top prospects' annual reports, or at least the letter from senior management that starts out every annual report. Do something to create leverage, and print the latest press releases of your major prospects off on your printer. Circle the Russian and Greek areas, and send them to your salespeople for them to act on. You will become a master at the languages in no time.

The final word about languages is the idea of staying the course of action you are currently on. Sales management has goals and objectives for its team, and most of them are goals based on revenue generation. Getting higher in the organization is a key factor in creating demand for your solutions, as well as getting decisions faster. Remember:

> *The trick is not calling high; anyone can do that. The trick*
>
> *is when you call high, what do you say?*

You now know.

The Final Word

Sales management, it is up to you to make changes. Make changes in your organization before they are needed, before the need for change becomes obvious to all but you. You need to make sure you have a learn and grow organization to stay on top year after year. Strategies are useful, but using tactics before strategies within a process wins out, every time.

Start right now with a PowerHour for yourself, and map out what you are going to do. Determine which RedZone customers do you want to have an immediate impact on, and set an example for the rest of the sales team? It's time for you to stop looking at the past, stop looking at reactive revenue metrics, and help your sales team on the ground at the point of attack, the sales call. It's time for you to become ProActive. Are you ready?

Appendix

ProActive Selling Tools

30-Second Speech

A brief conversation with the client where you learn about the client's needs and the client learns about you and your product. It will shift the seller from talking to listening in an easy and professional manner.

Buyers Buy Backwards (BBB)

Buyers have a fixed implementation date in mind, and work their schedule backwards from that date. Sellers always want to take progressive steps forward, which leads to a crossing of the two separate time agendas.

Decision Criteria (PPPII)

There are five reasons people buy: Product features, product quality, professional support, investment, and image. A seller needs to know the motivation for a buyer and should probe in these areas.

Flip

An open-ended question or comment that transfers the conversation to the other party. By doing this, the one who initiates the flip gains control of the conversation.

Implementation Date (I-Date)

The date by which your client needs your solution. This will drive the entire buy/sales process.

Implementation Plan (I-Plan)	A map that shows the client how you propose to move from the Implementation Date forward to a completed installation.
Three Languages	The three languages spoken by different levels of decision-makers. Managers are concerned with *Feature/Function.* Vice presidents are concerned with *Revenue/Cost.* Senior managers are concerned with *Market Share/Market Size.* Sellers need to understand all three languages and speak the right language at the appropriate time.
ProActive Sales Matrix	The ProActive Sales Matrix tells you what you should be doing and what zone you should be spending your time in.
PowerHour	One hour a day you set aside to exclusively work on your ProActive A accounts. It is a way to start your day in control of your schedule.
Three Levels of Why	The three reasons why people truly make buying decisions: Rapport, Rationalize, and Real.
SalesMap	Begins at the Educate step of the Sales Cycle and ends at the decision date. The entire journey you are going to describe to the client, and gain the client's agreement to, so you can pull the client through the sale one step at a time.
WarBook	A collection of facts and figures about your clients that will give you

more information about the clients than they know about themselves. A written strategic collection of information utilized to detail the important information that is affecting this sale. This is more than an account plan. A WarBook is done for the top sales potentials for the next few months.

Top Two Benefits   The top two reasons the buyer has expressed as to why he would buy your unique solution.

Towards/Away   The Buyer's motivational direction. Buyers are either Away from pain or Towards pleasure people.

Drop, Push, Pull   The three choices a salesperson can make at the end of Justify. Either Drop the prospect, Push to a close, or ProActively Pull to get an order.

Feature/Benefit/Value Selling   A way of educating a C level prospect. State the feature, the benefit, and then state the value the benefit is going to have for the prospect. It's better if prospects come up with the value on their own.

Institutional and Individual Reasons   The two reasons buyers make a decision. They have Individual and Institutional reasons. A ProActive salesperson needs to know both.

Time Demo   A process that walks a prospect forward in time to take ownership ProActively in your solution. A Time Demo is usually a nontransferable competitive exclusive.

Summarize, Bridge, and Pull (SBP)

A tool to use at the end of every sales call to make sure the prospect and the sales person are in agreement and want to continue on to a next step. With SBP, you are always pulling to the next step in the buy/sell process. It also identifies Dragons and reinforces the need for the buyer to make a decision.

Value Star

There are five ways to create value: ROI, Time, Risk, Motivation, and Brand. ProActive salespeople are always using the five points of the Star to create value in the prospect's mind.

ProActive Sales Management Tools

$R = F + C$

Revenue equals Frequency and Competency. These are the two ProActive variables sales managers can manage to.

M^2O/t

Mutually agreed upon measurable objectives over time. Objectives that work in a sales environment.

SOS Pyramid

The process to implement objectives: Situational analysis, setting Objectives, and then implementing a Strategy. The largest part of the Pyramid is the Situational analysis, and the smallest is the Strategy part.

Miller 17

The appraisal process that allows sales managers to be ProActive and mutually define and track Rs, Fs, and Cs.

Index